The
Butterfly
in You

MILT RODRIGUEZ

The Butterfly in You

DISCOVERING YOUR TRUE
IDENTITY IN CHRIST

THE BUTTERFLY IN YOU

Copyright ©2008 Milt Rodriguez

Published by

The Rebuilders admin@therebuilders.org/
www.therebuilders.org

Cover design and page layout by:
Rita Motta - Editora Tribo da Ilha - Brazil

Printed in the United States of America

Index

CATERPILLAR

COCOON

THE BUTTERFLY

Acknowledgments

There are several people who contributed to the formation of some of the ideas and thoughts in this book. They were all a definite influence in developing some of my understandings. T. Austin-Sparks, Watchman Nee, Gene Edwards, Bill Freeman, Frank Viola, and Chris Pridham all had a large part to play in the "Butterfly" story.

I would also like to express my heartfelt gratitude to those who contributed to the production of the book itself. Thanks to my beautiful wife for all her work in the typing of the manuscript. Thanks to Mike Biggerstaff, Jon Zens, and Frank Viola for their comments and editing of the manuscript.

Dedication

This book is dedicated to someone who is very dear to me. She has helped me to start and continue the journey into discovering my identity in Christ. And now, I have had the privilege of helping her to do the same. This book is dedicated to Nohemi Rodriguez. Thanks, Mom!

Foreword

The victorious Christian life. What is it, and can it be obtained in this life? Many Christian teachers say "yes," but it can only be obtained through hard work (they say). They teach that the Christian life is one of working toward victory.

This was the teaching that I cut my teeth on as a young believer. It bled through almost every sermon I heard and every book I read. "Try harder, and eventually, you will experience the victorious Christian life."

Like millions of other Christians, I've found this teaching to be tried and found wanting. I've yet to meet a Christian who proved it true in their own life. And in my observation, those who hold to it are still trying harder and waiting for the day when they will attain to that much desired but elusive victorious state.

To my mind, the major flaw in this teaching is that it begins with a wrong premise. The Christian life is not a matter of working *toward* victory by effort and hard labor. Instead, the Christian life is a matter of becoming who you already are. It's one of working *from* victory, not to it.

Milt Rodriguez has unraveled this very thought in *The Butterfly in You*. Written in a highly casual and conversational style, Milt attempts to present God's view of the believer's true identity.

If you are a Christian who wonders what God's opinion of you is... or if you're tormented by a guilt complex... or if you've been trying in vain to attain the victorious Christian life, then this book may be the right medicine to cure your troubled heart. It has the potential to set you on a different course—one where you no longer strive toward victory, but begin to live from it.

Frank Viola, author
Pagan Christianity and *Reimagining Church*
Gainesville, Florida

The Butterfly in You

Introduction

I pray that this book is used by the Lord as a tool of discovery. This "tool" is just one of the seeds along the journey of your discovering your true identity. This is a major need among believers in our day. We just don't know who we are. There is a major "identity crisis" among those who profess to know Jesus Christ.

Now we all know that people the world over have been speaking of an "identity crisis" for many years. Universally speaking, we have a need to know who we are. Why do I exist? What is the purpose of my life? Why was I born? These are questions that are being asked by both unbelievers *and* believers. I recently checked out the top ten best-selling books on Amazon.com, and eight out of ten of them were about your life is purpose. The tragedy is that believers actually have the answers, but don't even know it!

I strongly believe that a person cannot discover his/her true identity apart from Jesus Christ. Once you have him, you should know who you are. And yet, Christians *still* do not know who they are! This is our present sad situation. But why is this so? And how can it be remedied?

Faith Comes by Hearing

The first step is to believe who we are, instead of the falsehoods we have taken in. Right now, we believe in our *false* identity because of the lies we have been told. We have heard lies, and so that is what our faith is based upon. We have put our faith in lies.

The fact is that you have been lied to by the devil, the world system, the religious system, those around you who don't know any better, and yourself. First you must *hear* the truth, and then the truth will set you free. But you must also *believe* the truth — and therein lies the problem. Some of us have a hard time believing the truth about ourselves. But we still need to hear it before we can believe it. Faith comes by hearing.

That is why I have written this book. Someone needs to tell you the truth about your identity. But all I have done in this book is to take the scriptures about your identity and put them into my own words. I certainly did not make this stuff up.

But the problem is that we usually read the Bible with our "filtered" glasses on. If our filter is condemnation, then when we read the Scriptures we will feel condemned because we are not measuring up to God's holy standard. We read the Sermon on the Mount and we are condemned because we do not live like that. What does that tell me about myself? I am a miserable failure as a Christian because I cannot live up to that kind of lifestyle. So reading the Scriptures just reminds me of what a miserable failure and sinner I am. And why would I want to do that? But if I don't read the Bible, then I am also condemned because everyone knows that to be a good Christian you must know God's Word! So I am condemned either way.

Many believers find themselves caught in this unending cycle of condemnation and failure. But obviously, the problem is not with Scripture, but rather with our perception of what Scripture is saying.

Your only way out is by hearing the Truth. Jesus Christ, himself, is the Truth.

Simply put, you need to hear him.

You see, your true identity is inseparably interwoven into Jesus Christ. In other words, he *is* your identity! You can never truly know who you are without knowing him. Discover *his* identity and you will discover your own.

So that is my method of operation in this book. I launch out to show you the identity of your Lord. In doing so, my hope is that you will discover your own true identity within him. May you have a life-changing discovery.

PART ONE

Caterpillar

"Therefore from now on we recognize no one according to the flesh; even though we have known Christ according to the flesh, yet now we know him in this way no longer. Therefore if anyone is in Christ, he is a new creation; the old things have passed away; behold, new things have come."

2 Corinthians 5:16-17

Fred the Worm

ello.
"My name is Fred. I happen to be a worm.

"No, I mean that quite literally.

"I am an invertebrate, a worm. I was born that way a long time ago.

"This is who I am.

"I'm a worm. I'm Fred... the worm.

"I come from a long line of worms. My parents were worms, and their parents, and their parents.

"This is my destiny.

"This is my lot in life.

"I have never known anything else.

"One day while I was crawling through the weeds, foraging for some leaves to eat, I had a thought which I had never had before. This was a first. Thinking a new thought... wow! We worms just don't do that. We pretty much stick within the confines of the worm world and never think outside the weed patch, if you know what I mean.

"But here it was... a new thought. My little mind was pregnant with it. What if I could do something which I had never done before. What if I could stretch my long slinky body and actually lift my head up and off the ground. What would it feel like? What would I see? This was a scary thought.

"As far as I knew, no worm had ever done this before, or even thought about it! But here I was, thinking the unthinkable.

"So then, I decided I was actually going to follow through with this thought. I was going to stretch and lift my head up off the earth.

"I found an abandoned weed patch that had been eaten up. There was no one around and it was the perfect place. So I began the long process of pulling the muscles in every part of my long body to gather the strength to lift my head. Up and up went my head until I saw something so beautiful that I could hardly believe my squinty little eyes.

"What I saw appeared to be a massive blanket of blue stretching out above and around the old weed patch. It almost looked, for a moment, that the blue went on forever. But that, of course, is impossible. Nothing goes on forever. Every worm knows that!

"Well, from that day forward, I was on a mission. I had to discover what that blue stuff was because it was the most beautiful thing I had ever seen in my life.

"I crawled over to the next weed patch and asked around over there. But no one knew anything. In fact, they kind of acted like I was crazy for even asking. You see, we worms pretty much mind our own business. We are way too busy and reasonable to think about such crazy ideas. I mean, after all, we have to find our next patch of weeds to feed on. We keep our noses down to the ground so that we don't miss any leaves that could feed us for the next week or so. No one ever stretches like I did that day. There's no time for that. So I can understand why the other worms looked at me funny.

"But I know what I saw. And I just had to find out about the blue stuff. I don't know why.

"So I went back to my weed patch and decided to ask the old wise worm. Surely he would know. He told me that the blue stuff was called 'Up' but that it was only a legend and no one had actually ever proven its existence. As the legend goes, the 'Up' was a beautiful place - wonderful beyond imagination. It had no end. And there existed a race of creatures that could actually live and move in the Big Blue Up. But it was only a legend - the stuff of dreams and overactive imaginations.

"But yet... I knew what I had seen. And something inside of me was driving me on to find out more. I knew what I had to do. I would have to stretch again. But this time, I would stretch much further, as far as I could so that I could see more of the Big Blue Up.

"So I began stretching, further, and further, and further. Then my head turned and I could see it: the Big Blue Up. It was wonderful! And it did seem to go on forever. I couldn't take my eyes away from it, yet the stretching was becoming more difficult.

"Then, all of a sudden, I saw something move in the Big Blue Up. It looked like something alive but it was just out of my sight now. So I stretched even further to see this wonder. And when I did, my eyes beheld the most beautiful creature I had ever seen. It was covered with bright colors and was making some kind of fluttering movement. It was so fascinating to watch.

"Then, suddenly, it stopped moving and rested on a blade of grass. Now I could see its beauty even better... WOW! What a creature! The legends are all true! Then a thought entered my mind. I couldn't help myself. I just had to do it. I had to speak to him.

"What *are* you?" I asked.

"He turned his head downward and looked my way. 'I'm a Flyer,' he said. 'Yes, I live in the Big Blue Up.'

"Then I thought to myself, 'This is the perfect creature to live in the Big Blue Up. A glorious creature for a glorious place.' And then I thought, 'Oh well, what does that have to do with me?'

"Then, as if he read my thoughts, the Flyer spoke again. 'Fred, this is the place where you belong.'

'What? What are you *talking* about?'

"'Fred, you have the heart of a Flyer. In fact, the Flyer Life Seed has been placed within you. You *are* a Flyer!'

"My heart leapt within me at the sound of these words. Could it be, I wondered? Could it be true? Something within me got so excited at the possibility.

"But then I realized...

"Wait a minute, I'm just a worm. I was born a worm and I will always be a worm. What a stupid Flyer. He doesn't know anything. And besides, this stretching is really starting to get to me. Worms were never meant to stretch.

"I need to get back to my weed patch and scrounge up some leaves."

Fred sadly went back to business as usual. Little did he know that he really wasn't a worm at all.

He was a caterpillar.

The Need for Discovery

We believers today are very much like our little buddy, Fred the worm. We have many misconceptions about where we have come from, what we have, and where we are going. Yet these three things are essential for us to know in order for us to discover who we are. Jesus knew these three things, and so he was secure in his own identity.

> *Jesus, knowing that the Father had given all into his hands and that he had come forth from God and was going to God, rose from supper and laid aside his outer garments: and taking a towel, he girded himself...* (John 13: 3, 4).

The Lord could humble himself and wash the disciples' feet because he knew who he was. He knew that all things had been given to him by the Father. He knew that God was his origin and God was his destination. It was these "knowings" that gave him the foundation for his own identity. This identity was not based upon outward appearances or circumstances. It was only based upon established facts within the living God himself.

Fred the worm could only see things from an outward perspective. He thought that he came from a long line of worms and that his destiny was to eat leaves and mind his own business. He dared not even think any thoughts higher than that. He was a creature who was trapped within his own mindset; a prisoner of his own belief system and thought patterns. His "stretching" above those things was an incredibly courageous act.

Our Present Mindset

I believe that this is a picture of our situation among believers today. Most of us would dare not question the status quo or rock any religious boats. We just go about our daily business and never bother to "stretch" in order to discover a whole new world.

Our little friend, Fred, kept his nose to the ground and stayed in survival mode. He needed to provide for the next week's worth of groceries (weeds). This is the way that worms live. And Fred actually bought the lie that he was only a worm.

What about you, dear reader? What lies have you purchased? In the Garden of Eden, the serpent perpetrated a lie upon Eve. It wasn't an outright lie. That would be too obvious. It was an insinuation. This insinuation was a casting of doubt upon what God had done. He said, "You will be like God." Yet Eve (and Adam) had already been created in God's image. They were already like God.

But by the devil telling her that she could become like God, he put doubt into her mind that she was already like him. Do you see the slinky one's strategy? He attacked her identity. He threw into question who she was to get her to accept a lower position and then accept the lie that she would have to work her way back. In other words, she no longer accepted the fact that what God had done was enough. In order for her to become a complete person and be all that she should be, she now needed to do something (eat the fruit) in order to obtain her identity. She was trying to become something she already was.

What a deception. To try to attain an identity and a state of being that you already have. The enemy knew that her most vulnerable spot was her identity. And so, he has used that vulnerability ever since.

Hearing the Gospel

Our friend, Fred, actually believed the lie that he was a worm. His lot in life was only to find weed patches and eat. He kept his nose to the ground (grindstone) and never questioned his own identity. This is just like most believers today. This is just like you and me.

But one day Fred dared to think outside the box of systemic religion and had an epiphany. What if there was something more? What if I *am* something more? Then he saw the "Big Blue Up" and the beautiful creature that lived there. And then he heard the proclamation of the "Flyer."

"Fred, this is who you are!"

Internally, instinctively, Fred knew it was the truth. This was the Good News. This was the gospel. What is so ironic about this whole thing is that he knew it was the truth. However, he could not believe it. It was much easier to continue to believe the lie: "I am just a worm."

Fred desperately needed to know his true identity, but he refused to believe it. First of all, he needed to hear it spoken to him. Then he had to make his decision.

Unfortunately, we all live in a day when the truth about our identity is not being proclaimed very much at all. We could say that our true identity has been lost to silence. It's a hidden identity that has been lost to us. But without knowing your true identity and purpose, we will wander about aimlessly not knowing where we are going.

Most Christians today are in this condition. Therefore, we have had very little impact upon this creation, visible and invisible. We are just waiting for the next busload (weed patch) to heaven and are pretty much keeping our noses to the ground. We mind our own business and keep to ourselves. But God is trying to intervene. There is something that we desperately need to hear.

The Gospel.

We need to hear the truth about who Christ is, who we are, and the eternal purpose of God. This is the good news.

Dear believer, you are not a worm. Your purpose in life is not to keep your nose to the ground and just survive. You are so much more than that. I am here to tell you that you are a Flyer. You have been called to soar (and live) in the heavens.

This news must awaken you out of your "worm state." This news must shake you out of the lie and into reality. This news must shock you and rock your world. But most of all:

You must believe this wonderful news!

The first step in discovering your true identity is to know where you came from. Fred didn't know where he came from. He thought that he came from worms.

"*Blessed be the God and Father of our Lord Jesus Christ, who has blessed us with every spiritual blessing in the heavenly places in Christ, just as he chose us in him before the foundation of the world, that we would be holy and blameless before him.*"

Eph. 1: 3, 4

Chosen before Creation

You were never chosen to be a worm. A worm is a creature that crawls upon the ground without any legs. He crawls upon his belly all of his days. Sounds just like a serpent to me.

A worm will never become anything else except a worm. A worm will never leave the earth. A worm has no destiny. A worm was not chosen... he was cursed.

According to the letter written by the apostle Paul to the Ephesians, you and I were chosen by God the Father before the foundation of the world. This phrase "before the foundation of the world," is used several times in Scripture and it always means before there was anything. Before creation.

You were chosen before there was anything.

Have you ever thought about that? Before God created, he chose you. Before the Father created the invisible realm with all of the angels and all their glory . . . he chose you. Before he created the physical universe with all of the galaxies, solar systems, stars and planets... he chose you. Before he created the sky and the earth, the fish and the birds, the land and the ocean, the plants and the animals... he chose you.

He chose you before he created anything.

But what does it mean to be chosen? How and where did he choose you? The word "chosen" literally means to select, to be marked off, to hand pick. But what was there to hand select since nothing had been created yet?

The thought behind this "choosing" is as if you go to the produce section of a grocery store and "choose" some cantaloupes. You are *hand selecting* the melons you want. This is not just a mental or virtual choosing. This is not just a plan for the future. This is an actual choosing. God, the Father, actually hand selected you and me. But what did he select us from? To answer that question, we must see the location of his choosing.

In Ephesians, Paul tells us the specific location where God chose us. But wait a minute. Nothing has been created yet. How could there be any locations? There could be only one. And that location had not been created.

The Father chose us inside his Son!

He chose us inside this wonderful, uncreated location called... in Christ. This location is the eternally living Son of God. The Father hand picked you inside his Son before there was anything.

This answers the question of *where,* but what about the question of *what?* In our little illustration of the produce, it was the cantaloupes. But what is it here, inside of Christ? Now picture the Father standing inside of Christ. What does he see? There could be only one substance. It is the divine life of the Son himself! The only thing the Father sees all around him is the vibrant, glorious, eternal life of the Son of God. This is his "choosing ground." This is his "produce" from which to choose. He "marked off" some of the life of the Son and held it in reserve as a seed. This is the part of divine life that would be placed into you at some point. Paul tells us in 1 Cor. 12:12 that we are members or 'parts' of Christ. These parts were chosen by the Father before creation.

Eternal Life for You

I came that you might have life... (John 10:10).

Eternal life is God's life, divine life. It is uncreated because it is God himself. In essence, when God gives us his life, he is giving us himself. This is the part of life reserved for us in his Son.

The Father chose you before creation. He hand picked a part of his Son and placed your name on it. It was "reserved" for you, so to speak. Then, he created all things. He created time and at some point, you came along. At the point in your life when you turned to him, that's when he placed that "reserved" portion of Christ into you.

God's Idea of Adoption

> *He predestined us to adoption as sons through Jesus Christ to himself, according to the kind intention of his will, to the praise of the glory of his grace, which he freely bestowed on us in the Beloved* (Eph. 1:5, 6).

When God chose you, he adopted you as his child through his Son, Jesus Christ. This is not adoption as we know it in this world. You were not an abandoned child that no one wanted and God felt sorry for you, so he took you in. God's adoption is not that way at all. However, he did *choose* you to be his own special child. Unlike natural adoption, this holy adoption includes a *real* choosing and a *real* giving of life.

In natural adoption, you choose a child who is an orphan but that child never really becomes your blood relative. Not so with God's adoption. He chose you before creation by hand selecting a portion of the life of his Son. In other words, he chose you out of his very own DNA pool. This "pool" is Christ.

This is why you can cry "Abba, Father" and really mean it (Rom. 8:15). It's because you have the same DNA as God, the Father. This was chosen for you in Christ before creation.

Isn't this wonderful? What a God we have!

This magnificent God actually stopped everything he was doing to take quality time and engage himself in a very special event:

Your choosing.

Before there was anything, he chose you. Can you see his priorities? Before he created one thing, he wanted to settle this thing about who and what you are, and what your destiny would be. He placed everything on hold until he accomplished this great task. The Father "walked into" the warehouse of his life contained within his Son. Then he carefully chose a part of that divine, eternal life and joyfully marked off that special part of Christ that would one day be placed inside of you.

> *He chose you in Christ before the foundation of the world that you would be holy and blameless before him* (Eph. 1:4 [paraphrased]).

"Hi again. This is Fred the worm. The day I was born something very peculiar happened. I completely forgot everything. I was born with no recollection of anything. In fact, I still can't even remember being born at all. I have to take the word of others for it.

"But the day I was born I came into this world with a sort of total amnesia. I had forgotten where I came from.

I had forgotten what I had been given. And I had forgotten where I was headed. I had completely forgotten what happened to me *before* creation. I had completely forgotten that I was chosen in Christ sometime during eternity past. I had also forgotten that I was slain inside the Lamb before creation (Heb. 13:8).

"But now I am beginning to remember all of these things. And I am beginning to remember the most wonderful thing of all: my place inside the living God! I am beginning to remember that place where no words could possibly describe the flow of life and love and sacrifice. That place where the love of God is produced and flows like a mighty river. That place where the Father loves the Son without hindrance and the Son loves the Father in return. That place where life and love are shared in the divine ocean of the Spirit."

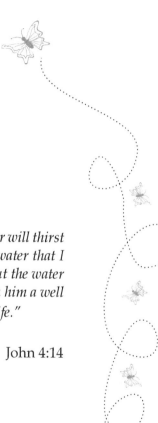

"Everyone who drinks of this water will thirst again; but whoever drinks of the water that I will give him shall never thirst; but the water that I will give him will become in him a well of water springing up to eternal life."

John 4:14

New Birth

It goes without saying that something incredibly amazing happened to you when you came to Christ. You were born "from above" or born anew. However, neither the Scriptures, nor theology, can fully describe what happened inside you at that time.

We try, in our feeble ways, to describe and explain what happens at new birth, but it never really measures up to the reality of it all. Because we are talking about divine, eternal things here, it is difficult to put our fingers on it. When you were regenerated, it was the result of two decisions: yours and God's. God chose you before creation, and you chose him in time and space. Because of your turning to him, he took that life of his Son that was chosen before creation and placed it inside you.

But how did God know you would choose him? Remember, he chose *you* before creation. He "hand selected" a particular part of the life of his Son that would be his unique expression through you. Does this mean that he predestined you? Yes, most definitely. Does that mean that you had no choice in the matter? No, it does not. You always have your free will. It is a gift from God and he never takes it away.

You see, he chose you because you chose him. And you chose him because he chose you. Our God lives outside of time and space. He is not confined by such things. He sees the beginning and the end and everything in between, all at the same time. The words "before" and "after" really lose their meaning in eternity. God can see that you chose him *within* time and then decide to choose you *before* time began. Of course, this was all initiated by him and he drew you to himself by his spirit.

There was a moment in time when you gave your life to him. At that very moment, the Father took that part of Christ that he chose before creation and placed it inside you. At that very moment, you became a new creation.

The Seed

There are many places in scripture where Christ is referred to, literally and figuratively, as the seed (Gen. 1: 11-12; Gen 3:15; Ps. 89:4; Is. 55:10; Matt. 13:31; Gal. 3:16; 1 Pet. 1:23; 1 John 3:9). The life of Christ that the Father chose before creation is placed inside of you at your conversion. This life of the Son acts like a seed within you. In other words, the Father placed his very own Son within you.

> *Christ in you, the hope of glory...* (Col. 1:27b).

God has placed the seed of his Son within you. It is so easy for me to pen these words, yet this must take center stage in your heart, mind, and spirit. This must become the life altering revelation that changes everything for you.

Christ in you.

These cannot be just words. This must be life. This must be revelation to you. Without the Holy Spirit making this real to you, it will be just dead doctrine. It will produce absolutely nothing.

It seems to me that most believers today do not have this revelation. To them, "Christ in you" is only a doctrine.

Yes, of course, the scriptures teach this, so we all agree with it. But do we really believe it? What about you? Do you actually believe that the Son of God lives within you?

Paul of Tarsus came to a point in his life when God, the Father, revealed this to him.

> *But when it pleased God, who set me apart from my mother's womb and called me through his grace, to reveal his Son in me that I might announce him as the gospel among the Gentiles...* (Gal. 1: 15, 16a).

But, unfortunately, most of us are like Fred the worm. We actually believe that we are worms. This is because we do not know that there is a seed of another life inside of us. That seed is what makes all the difference between a worm and a caterpillar. A worm is just a worm. He will always be a worm. But a caterpillar has the life seed of a butterfly within him! He is destined for greatness because of the life dwelling in him.

Dear one, you are not destined to grovel around in the dirt looking for weed patches all your life. You have a wonderful and glorious destiny because of the life seed that lives within you.

The Location of the Seed

Knowing that Christ lives within you is a wonderful discovery, but it must go further than that. First, you need to have a revelation that he lives inside you. Then you need to understand what that means practically. The seed of the living God is dwelling inside you... but where? The

Father deposited the seed of his Son into a specific location in your being. That location is called your spirit. You are a tripartite being that is composed of a spirit, a soul, and a body.[1] Your spirit is the innermost part of you. It is the part of you that was given to contain the life of God.

The Seed is Spirit

> *So also it is written, 'the first man, Adam, became a living soul.' The last Adam became a life-giving spirit* (1 Cor. 15:45).

After Jesus was resurrected, he became a life-giving spirit. He appeared to the disciples in a shut-up room, breathed on them, and said, "Receive the Holy Spirit" (John 20:22). When that happened, Christ came to live in the spirit of each of the disciples. He, as the life-giving spirit, entered into the spirit of each disciple by means of the Holy Spirit. The Spirit-seed was planted into the spirit of each disciple in the room.

Now if this wasn't tremendous enough, something even more glorious happened! The Spirit that was planted into each disciple actually became one with the spirit of that disciple. In other words, when the seed was planted into you, his Spirit became one with your spirit (1 Cor. 6:17).

Imagine filling up a glass with water and then dropping three drops of red food coloring into the glass. What color is the water now? Red. Is the liquid now water or food coloring? It is a new liquid which is a combination of both.

---

[1] See the author's book *"The Temple Within"*

Can you now separate the water from the red food coloring? No, they are one. Are there now two liquids in the glass? No, there is only one. This is what happened when God's Spirit came to live in your spirit. The two became one. You cannot separate them. There is now no distinction between his Spirit and your spirit. You have become one with Jesus Christ.

If this doesn't get you excited, then you better check your pulse!

He has truly changed water into wine. He has made you like him: a person who has both human life *and* divine life.

The Birthing of Christ

> *My children, with whom I am again in labor*
> *until Christ is formed in you...* (Gal. 4:19).

It could be said that your spirit is like a womb for Christ. Just as Mary of Nazareth physically had Jesus living inside her, so you spiritually have him inside you.

He is growing and maturing inside your spirit. God's desire is that Christ would grow in you to the point of permeating your spirit, then your soul, and then your body. He is one with your spirit, but he wants to expand into your soul - the mind, will, and emotions. This happens by your choosing to live by his life within you instead of your own life on a daily basis.

> *I have been crucified with Christ; and it is no*
> *longer I who live, but Christ lives in me; and*
> *the life which I now live in the flesh I live by*

> *the faith of the Son of God, who loves me and*
> *gave himself up for me* (Gal. 2:20).

This Christ who lives within you desires a visible expression. The Father placed the seed of his Son inside of you so that his life would be expressed and expanded by a whole new race.

You are an important part of that new race.

"I cannot help myself...
The way that I am, I'm more harm than good to me...
And I can't accept myself...
As far as I am from the place I want to be.
You do not offer help...
Not even remotely interested... in making me better
But You want a whole new creation...
That requires the annihilation of me
And You want my old life to lay down and die so that You...
So that You can live in me."

Charlie Dodrill
New Creation
from the CD
Prologue to this Drama

The New You

red was a caterpillar, not a worm. The look, function, and purpose of a caterpillar is completely different from that of a worm. But the most important difference is that the caterpillar has entirely different "insides" than a worm.

Many Christians actually believe that they are dirty rotten sinners and they are here on earth to survive as best they can until they die and go "home" to heaven. I have even heard believers, when confronted with their true identity in Christ, retort by saying that their true identity is *Sinner!*

Sinner or Saint?

What about you, dear reader? Do you also believe that you are a sinner? Well, if you do, I am here to prove you wrong. You *were* a sinner, but now you are a *saint.*

> But God demonstrated his own love toward us, in that while we were yet sinners, Christ died for us (Rom. 5:8).

Notice the phraseology in this scripture: "while we *were* yet sinners." Christ died for us *when* we *were* sinners. But we are no longer sinners. We were at one time. That's when he died for us, when we were still in that state. But now we are different. Now we are in a new place. Now we are in Christ and Christ is in us. Oh yes, it's true that we may sin at times. But we are no longer sinners. We no longer have a sin nature. We have been freed from the power of sin. Now we can choose to sin or not to sin. We are no longer slaves to sin. The old man has been crucified with Christ. Sin no longer has any power over us. This is the wonderful message given to us by Paul in Romans 5, 6, and 7.

When the Saints Come Marching In

So, if you are no longer a sinner, then what are you? You are a saint! The Bible says that you are a "holy one." This may be hard for you to accept at first. But it is the gospel truth. You don't have to be "canonized." If you are a believer in the Lord Jesus Christ, then you are already a saint.

But you may be wondering about all those bad things you have done. A saint wouldn't do those things. How could this be? Let me tell you what a saint is and how it is possible that you have become one.

The word "saint" literally means 'a holy one.' But what does it mean to be holy? The term "holy" means to be separated or set apart to God and his purpose. Whatever is holy is no longer common but is now "special" in the sense of being separated for God. Because of what Jesus accomplished on the cross, you have been separated and set apart for God. You are his possession. You are a holy one. It doesn't depend upon what *you* do. It depends upon what *he* already has done. That is something called grace.

Grace or Law

For the law was given through Moses; grace and reality came through Jesus Christ (John 1:17).

Many Christians believe that they are still dirty rotten sinners and they therefore need to repent every minute of every day. These believers still live under a mountain of guilt from their past. They have not fully received the completed work of Jesus Christ that he accomplished on the cross. They somehow believe that his work on the cross is incomplete. When he said, "It is finished," he was just kidding. Now we, the sinners, must atone for our own sins by repenting, repenting, repenting, *ad infinitum*. These poor Christians are still functioning under the Old Covenant law of Moses. They are still living in condemnation and guilt.

> *There is now then no condemnation to those who are in Christ Jesus. For the law of the Spirit of life has freed me in Christ Jesus from the law of sin and death* (Rom. 8:1, 2).

These believers either have never read or they have never understood the message of the letter to the Hebrews. In chapter ten, the writer deals with this issue of sin (and sacrifices for sin, i.e. "repentance") once and for all.

> *For by one offering he has perfected forever those who are being sanctified. And the Holy Spirit also testifies to us, for after having said, 'This is the covenant which I will covenant with them after those days, says the Lord: I will impart my laws upon their hearts, and upon their mind I will inscribe them,' He then says, 'And their sins and their lawlessness I shall by no means remember anymore'* (Heb. 10:14 - 17).

The problem is that even though God has forgotten our sins, we have not. Many cannot completely receive God's forgiveness and so feel that they need to do something to pay for the sins themselves. Sorry. That's not God's way. He already did all the work and paid the price for your sins. You *are* forgiven. You *are* clean. You *are* holy. Not because of *your* holiness but because of his. Now, he *is* your holiness.

Many Christians have still only believed in the baptism of John (the Baptist) which is a baptism of repentance. They have not moved on to the baptism of Christ. Paul ran into a group of believers like this in Ephesus (see Acts 19: 1-7). We don't want to hang onto John once we have met Jesus.

The Need for Repentance

Now please don't misunderstand me. I am not saying that there is never a need for a Christian to repent. Actually, the term "repentance" in the original language means "to turn." We should be constantly *turning* to the Lord. There are times in our lives when we have sinned and turned away from the Lord and we definitely need to repent (turn back to him). But the focus should *always* be him, not the sin. If we are always thinking about not sinning, guess what we will do. Sin.

We want to see as he sees. And he sees us as holy, blameless, and above reproach (Eph. 1:1 - 4).

This is why Paul uses the term "saints" to greet the believers in the various churches (See: 1 Cor. 1:2; 2 Cor. 1:1; Eph. 1:1; Phil. 1:1; Col. 1:2).

The Two Men

You need to be able to see yourself from God's viewpoint. His perspective is really the only one that counts.

Wouldn't you agree? So the key here is to capture his perspective on your identity.

As far as God is concerned, there are only two men in the whole universe. Those two men are the first Adam and the last Adam.

> *So also it is written, 'the first man, Adam, became a living soul. The last Adam became a life-giving spirit'* (1 Cor. 15:45).

You were originally born into the first Adam. You were part of Adam's race. You were born a sinner. But then you received Christ and were transferred from the 'old' humanity to the 'new' humanity. You were brought from the first Adam to the last Adam, who is Christ. Now you no longer have any identity in the first Adam. Your only identity now is in Christ. You are part of the "new Creation." You are a member of the "new man."

Your identity is now based on that of the new man, the last Adam, who is Christ. You are now dead to the first Adam. You can no longer take the thoughts, feelings, attitudes, actions, and lifestyle from that old race. It just doesn't fit who you are. And if you try to do that, it just won't work because you no longer belong to that race. Yet, we all try to do that, don't we? We all still believe that our identity is based upon the first Adam. Let me ask you a series of five questions to prove my point. Answer them as honestly as possible.

1) Do you believe that your identity is determined by what you do? Does doing determine being? Does your career define you? Does what you do every day determine who you are? Remember the age-old

question: "What do you want to be when you grow up?"

2) Do you believe that your identity is established by your relationship to other people? Are you a mother or a father? Are you a husband or a wife? Do these relationships define who you are? Ever heard of the "empty nest syndrome"? This is when a woman (or man) becomes emotionally distraught and depressed because her children have grown and left the home. Her whole identity was wrapped up in her kids.

3) Do you believe that your identity was given to you by your parents? "I have become my mother!" is an exclamation that women sometimes make. And men say, "I have become my father!" Are you the sum total of how you were raised? Do genetics determine who you are?

4) Do you believe that your circumstances determine your identity? You have been burned and abused by other people, even by other Christians. You have gone through some hard times financially. You lost three jobs and your wife left you. Are these circumstances who you are? Are you a helpless victim of your environment?

5) Do you believe that your decision determines your identity? You have (perhaps) made many mistakes in your life. Does that mean you are a failure? Do your choices determine who you are?

Is it not true that most of us derive our sense of identity from one or more of these five areas? But don't be fooled.

None of these things define who you are. You are now part of a "new humanity," the last Adam. All of your identity comes from that new position.

The Masterpiece

In Ephesians chapter two, Paul gives us a wonderful description of how our position (and corresponding identity) completely changed.

I suggest that you read Ephesians 2 right now and then come back to this book.

Can you see who you *were?* You *were* dead in your trespasses and sins. You *were* a son of disobedience. You *were* a child of wrath. You *were* living in the lusts of your flesh and indulging yourself in those lusts of body and mind.

But God...

Made you alive with Christ.

Raised you up with Christ.

Seated you in heavenly places with Christ.

So that he might show (display) the surpassing riches of his grace in kindness toward us in Christ.

For you are his masterpiece!

Created to perform good works.

The word "masterpiece" in the Greek literally is *poiema* which means something which has been handcrafted or composed, such as a poem. This is an artistic expression of the life and nature and character of the artist.

This is so God could have a visible expression of his love and grace and mercy to show all who are in both the visible and invisible worlds.

"Fullness is our permanent state. Fullness is our real situation. Are you not in Christ? Is your spirit not intertwined and joined with the One in whom dwells all the fullness of the Godhead bodily? Are you not right now joined to Christ in your spirit? Now, who will you relate to when you wake up in the morning? Will you relate to the self, with all the thoughts and feelings of the soul life? Or will you relate to your real life?

When you relate to Christ, your real life, you relate to your state of fullness."

Bill Freeman
All the Fullness
The Christian
Vol. 14, No. 10

The Fullness of Christ

He is the image of the invisible God, the first-born of all creation, because in him all things were created, in the heavens and on the earth, the visible and the invisible, whether thrones or lordships or rulers or authorities; all things have been created through him and unto him. And he is before all things, and all things were in him; and he is the head of the body, the church; he is the beginning, the firstborn from the dead, that he himself might have the first place in all things. For in him all the fullness was pleased to dwell (Col. 1: 15 - 19).

The best way for me to describe to you the identity you have in Christ is by describing your wonderful Lord. *He* is your true identity. *He* is your real life now (Col. 3:4). You have no other life now except Christ (Phil. 1:21).

I would ask you to recall our little story at the beginning of this book about Fred. Notice that Fred was not told that he was a worm or even a caterpillar. He was told that he was a Flyer. Why? He sure looked like a worm. He was crawling on the ground looking for weed patches. He sure lived the life of a worm.

Similarly, we are told constantly that we are worms. You and I have been told by our friends, family, society, and ourselves that we are born to crawl on the ground and that is really who we are. This flying stuff is just a silly legend.

But that is not what Fred was told by the Flyer himself.

The Flyer told Fred the truth. And Fred could see his true identity by looking at the Flyer! This is how you will discover *your* true identity. You must look at Christ and only then will you discover who you are. Let's take a panoramic view of this wonderful Christ.

The Bank Account of the Father

When we try to describe the fullness of Christ we tend to really fall short of an adequate supply of words. This is an area which is definitely too immense for the limitations of language. So I am going to use the illustration of a bank account. I believe most of us are familiar with having and managing a bank account.

Let's think of God, the Father, as having his own bank account. This bank account is his only begotten Son, Jesus Christ. The Father has been depositing (or investing) into this account for a long time. Let's take a look at what he has deposited.

The Image of God

What do the scriptures mean when they speak of Jesus Christ being the "image" of God? An image is a representation of something. If I take a photograph of someone, then that picture is a representation or a reminder of that person. The photo is not the person. It is simply a sign or likeness of that person. This is our idea of an image.

But God's idea of an image is much more intense. To God, an image is not just a representation or a clone. The image is the same as the person. The image is alive with the same life as the actual person. In other words, the image is the embodiment of the person.

God, the Father, is spirit. He is invisible to this visible (physical) realm. But Christ makes him visible. Christ is the visible embodiment of the invisible God. He is actually God made visible; God in the flesh. The Father has deposited everything into his Son so that the Son could visibly display all that is in the Father. If you have seen the Son, then you have seen the Father (John 14: 8, 9). That's because the Father and the Son are one.

The image gives us the concept of visible expression. The Father wants to be visibly expressed. He does this through and in his Son.

The Firstborn of All Creation

Christ is called the firstborn of creation because all things were created through him, to him, and in him. In this section of this passage, Paul is referring to the old creation, the creation of the visible and invisible universe.

All the stars, planets, galaxies and universes were created in your Lord. What a huge Christ we have. He is so much bigger than what we have thought. Not only the physical universe, but also the invisible universe was created in him. This includes the angels and the heavenly places. This includes many invisible places that are yet to be discovered and are yet untold. These, too, were created in Christ, through Christ, and to Christ.

This is why, in creation, you can see beautiful pictures of Christ. The artist cannot paint something without placing something of himself/herself into the work of art. When we look around us we can't help but see wonderful reflections of him. Just as the moon reflects the light of the sun, so does the Son reflect all the glory of the Father.

Do you see how much God has deposited into his bank account? What a rich Lord we have! But there is still much more...

All Things Hold Together in Him

You could say that Christ is the "glue" that holds the universe together. He is the center of all things. The force of gravity is a picture of him. Everything on this planet only stays put on this planet because of the force of gravity. And gravity comes from the center of the earth. I don't understand how it works, but somehow, everything is being pulled toward the center of the earth. That is the only reason why things don't fly off the surface of the earth and go floating about in space.

Christ is the *real* gravity. He is constantly pulling all things toward himself. He is the *true* center of the universe. And all things, and places, and persons "gravitate" to him.

And the Father's bank account continues to grow...

The Head of the Body

Paul tells us here that Christ, himself, is the actual living head of the body, the church. In Ephesians chapter one, Paul tells us what God's plan is for the fullness of the times; to head up all things in Christ (Eph. 1:10). This includes the things in heaven and the things on earth.

God has made Christ the head of the church so that he might fulfill his plan of bringing all things in the universe under his headship, that Christ would be the sum total of all positive things in the universe. God has deposited all his authority and power into his Son.

My! How this bank account is growing.

Firstborn from the Dead

Paul is now speaking of the *new* creation. "He is the beginning, the firstborn from the dead..." means the resurrection of Christ. He is the seed, the firstborn of a whole new race. He has the first place in all things in this new humanity. He is the preeminent one. He is not just number one. But rather, he has the primary place in everything. In each and everything, he is first.

> *He is firstborn among many brothers...*
> (Rom. 8:29b).

This is just a small glimpse into the fullness of the Father's bank account. This Christ is so much more than that.

Do you see how much God has invested into his Son? Can you see a little bit of his fullness?

IN HIM ALL THE FULLNESS WAS PLEASED TO DWELL

His Son contains the following:
♦ the old creation
♦ the universe, visible and invisible
♦ time
♦ space
♦ all planets, solar systems, galaxies, environments
♦ eternity past
♦ eternity future

♦ God's eternal purpose
♦ the new creation
♦ the church (the holy ones)
♦ the kingdom (reign and rule of God)
♦ and much more!

But the most astounding fact in all this is the all-inclusive Christ lives inside of you! He has actually become one with you. There is now no separation between you and him. You are one with him just as he is one with his Father.

Please take some time right now to let this fact sink into your spirit. It will take you the rest of eternity to fully experience it.

"But we all, with unveiled face, beholding as in a mirror the glory of the Lord, are being transformed into the same image from glory to glory, just as from the Lord, the Spirit."

2 Cor. 3:18

Preparing for Chrysalis (Cocoon)

Fred believes that he is a worm. He doesn't know that he is actually a caterpillar. None of the other caterpillars have told him this. Probably because they don't know it themselves! The existence of a glorious creature called a "Flyer" is just a myth or legend. Even though it is mentioned in the ancient writings, no one really believes in it. No, a worm is a worm is a worm.

But some of the worm population actually believes that a worm can change into something else. A worm can become better. A worm can improve himself. Can a cat become a dog? Can a bird become a giraffe? Can a worm become a caterpillar?

Do People Change?

A close brother in the Lord asked me this question recently. I have to admit that at first, I had no idea how to answer him. But then, it came rolling out of my mouth and surprised everyone, including me.

"No. People do not change."

It rang true in my spirit when I said it, yet I didn't know why. The other brothers disagreed with me and then one brother went on to explain why. He explained that he had seen many people change and that even non-believers can change.

But I suppose it depends upon how you define "change." Yes, I agree that people can change their behavior. A criminal can stop committing crimes. An alcoholic can stop drinking. An obese person can stop overeating. But isn't this just a change in behavior? Sure, we can all change our behavior simply by using the power of our will. But does this really change who we are? Does this change the deep core of our identity?

I'm sure that you have heard it said that someone with an addictive personality will always be an addict. Even if you completely stop the heroin or alcohol, you will always be an addict or alcoholic. Changing the behavior does not change who you are. You are a part of Adam's race. You are a fallen person, a sinner.

However, when you come to Christ, you are transferred from Adam's race into a whole new race. This is the race of the last Adam, Christ. The sinner has become a saint. The lost has become found. The miserable failure has become a masterpiece. The worm has become a caterpillar.

Ah, so a worm *can* become a caterpillar. Yes, but not by anything the worm did. It was all because of what God did. You see, the worm had to die and then be reborn as a caterpillar. This is not a change . . . this is a new creation. God didn't try to change Adam and "fix him up." He created a whole *new* race.

Caterpillars Trying to Change into Butterflies

The sad situation today is that believers just don't know who they are in Christ. So we are always trying to become something that we already are. We are working hard at becoming better mothers, fathers, businessmen, employees, neighbors, etc. We are hard at work trying to become better Christians. We pray more, give more, read the Bible more, witness more, etc. All in hopes of becoming good Christians. All in hopes of becoming saintly. But we are *already* saints. We are *already* holy. We are *already* blameless. We are *already* pure and spotless and without blemish. We are *already* pleasing to God. We are already in the Canaan land. We are in Christ. This is the deception of all deceptions. To try and become something we already are. To attempt to get some place we already are.

We have *already* been crucified with him. We have *already* been resurrected with him. We have *already* been ascended with him. And we are *right now* seated with him in the heavenlies (see Eph. 2:5, 6).

We do not have to attain any position or status with God. We are in Christ and Christ is in us. We are one with him. What other position could we possibly attain? What more could we possibly become than we already are? This gross misunderstanding has led us down a path which leads to scores of believers who are barking up the wrong trees.

Why do you think that God has placed his Son inside you? So that you could change yourself into a better person? So that you could become a better caterpillar?

No. The secret of the caterpillar lies *within* the caterpillar.

Metamorphosis

But what about being transformed into his image? What about growing up and becoming a mature son of God? Aren't all of these things discussed in the Scriptures?

Yes, but unfortunately our understanding of them is only taken in light of our present "self-improvement" concepts.

The Bible has a term that it uses to describe this maturation process of the believer. The word is "transformation." This word in the literal Greek is *"metamorphoo."* Sound familiar? It should. We derive out word "metamorphosis" from it. It can also be translated as transfiguration. It means to undergo a radical change from one form to another. This is the process which takes place as a caterpillar becomes a butterfly.

But this "change" or metamorphosis does not happen as you may think. It doesn't happen because you change yourself (with God's help). You can never change who you are deep down inside. It doesn't happen because God points out one of your faults and then tells you to "work on it." This is not the way of transformation at all.

Let's take a look at the life of a caterpillar/butterfly and the life of our Lord to find the answer.

"He must increase, but I must decrease."

John 3:30

The Secret of Metamorphosis

W e can see a small glimpse of the reality of metamorphosis at one point in the life of our Lord. I
am referring to what is commonly called his "transfiguration." The same root word is used in the original language
for both "transformation" and "transfiguration." That
word is *metamorphoo.*

But what actually happened when the Lord took Pe-
ter, James, and John to the mountain and his face shone
like the sun and his garments became as white as light (see
Matt. 17: 1-13)? Some of the glory of God peeked through
the flesh of Jesus Christ. This was a preview of the kingdom coming in all of its glory. The kingdom of God always
comes from within and then shines out through us. From
heaven to earth. From spirit to flesh.

Jesus was revealing the glory of the Father within
him. That wonderful divine life within him (who is the Father) was exposed in a very small measure in all his power
and glory. Any more than that and the disciples would not
have been able to handle it.

But this event shows us how metamorphosis works.
The life within breaks forth and is expressed without. God
works his way out of us. Of course, he never leaves us, but
he wants to be expressed in and through us. He wants to
be made visible through human flesh. He wants to express
himself through our personalities and lives.

Right now you have the divine life and nature of the
living God inside of you. The *real you* that I have been describing in this book resides within your spirit, your innermost

being. In the deepest part of you, there lives a whole new creation. That person is you and Christ as one. That person is the *you* version of Christ. That person *is* already everything you've always wanted to be. That person has all the qualities and character of Jesus Christ. That person is holy and blameless and righteous. That person is bold and confident, and yet loving and humble. That person loves God with all of his being and completely trusts, obeys, and believes. That person is:

"Christ in you, the hope of glory."

And this person wants to come out and express himself. That's where "glory" comes in. The glory is the expression of the life of God. The hope of this expression taking place is this wonderful Person living inside of you. The process of this Person breaking forth is called transformation (metamorphosis).

It doesn't happen by you gritting your teeth and working real hard to change your outward behavior. The transformation takes place as you yield to the life within and allow it to be expressed through you. You already have the beautiful butterfly living within you. You already are a new person inside. Now you just need to cooperate with the Holy Spirit to release the butterfly from within.

Did you know that a caterpillar sheds his skin five times before the chrysalis is revealed?

> *Therefore we do not lose heart, but though our outer man is decaying, yet our inner man is being renewed day by day. For momentary, light affliction is producing for us an eternal weight of glory far beyond all comparison, while we look not at the things which are*

> seen, for the things which are seen are tem-
> poral, but the things which are not seen are
> eternal (2 Cor. 4:16 - 18).

The caterpillar sheds his skin to reveal the butterfly within. However, something else happens during metamorphosis. The caterpillar enters into a new environment. This environment is the pupal stage (chrysalis) where the butterfly is fully developed. This is the cocoon from which the butterfly is born.

The Corporate Cocoon

God has already provided a "cocoon" environment for you. This is the natural habitat where you can break out of the old life and be who you were always meant to be. This is the atmosphere in which you can show your true colors.[2]

This metamorphosis is something that you do not experience alone. You see, the full expression of your true identity in Christ is not only an individual matter. This is something that you must go through with other saints. This is because your full identity is inextricably linked together with your brothers and sisters in Christ.

The Increase of Christ

One day, some disciples of John the Baptist came and told him that Jesus and his disciples were baptizing more people than they. It's very interesting to see how John answered them (John 3: 26 - 31).

---

[2] See the author's book *The Coat of Many Colors*

First, he tells them that no man can receive anything unless it has been given to him from heaven. Then he reminds them that he is not the Christ, but only a forerunner of Christ.

Second, he tells them that the one who possesses the bride is the bridegroom (Christ). But the friend of the bridegroom (John) hears him and rejoices at hearing his voice.

Third, he tells them, "He must increase, but I must decrease."

Now it is this third part that completely baffles us. Most people take this as a completely individual matter. To most, this passage is all about John's ministry and Jesus' ministry. John was saying that his ministry must decrease and the ministry of Jesus must take over. But that is not what the text says.

"He must increase, but I must decrease."

You can clearly see by the pronouns being used that this is not about ministries. This is about two persons. *He* must increase, but *I* must decrease. The first question we must ask is: Who is this person who must increase? Who is *he*?

The answer is given to us in the previous verse (29). This person is the bride and bridegroom. He is the one who is made up of *both* the bridegroom *and* the bride. He is the one who is made up of both the head *and* the body. He is the one new man that Paul spoke of (Eph. 2:15-16). He is the whole Christ, the all-inclusive Christ, the Corporate Christ (Col. 3:10-11).

And the bride is his increase. Christ is expanded and enlarged through his bride. She gives him expression and increase. You see, he is so much bigger than you ever thought possible. You and I are the increase of Christ! You and I are parts of his bride, of his body. This is absolutely wonderful.

Now, I hope that you can see that there is really only one caterpillar. And we are all parts of that one caterpillar. This is not just about you. This is about *us.* Christ is made up of head *and* body. And we are all his body. And in order for him to fully get his expression (butterfly), we must be in the right environment.

PART TWO

Cocoon

"Consequently, Paul understood that Christ is no longer an individual man. Rather, he is a corporate man... a corporate body that includes many members. This new knowing of Christ is knowing him as the church. 'If any man is in Christ, he is a new creation.' Knowing this new creation is to know Christ. Not after a human viewpoint, but after God's viewpoint."

Frank Viola
God's Ultimate Passion

The Environment of the Cocoon Life

The butterfly cannot be released without the proper environment. The cocoon provides everything the caterpillar needs to allow the growth and release of the butterfly within.

The Renewing of the Mind

The first step in this process takes place in your own mind. That mind needs to be renewed, as the Scriptures say. Up to this point you have thought that *you* were the caterpillar. You have thought that you were a separate, isolated individual and were living the "individual Christian life." You applied all of the Scriptures to your own individual life. You were consumed with your own individual relationship to God and the growth of that relationship. But now someone is telling you that you are not the caterpillar. That you are only *part* of the caterpillar and that all believers make up this one corporate caterpillar. How will your mind adjust to this proclamation? Will you allow your own mindset to be cracked wide open and a new one to enter in?

> *Do not lie to one another, since you have put off the old man with his practices and have put on the new man, which is being renewed unto full knowledge according to the image of him who created him, where there cannot be*

> *Greek and Jew, circumcision and uncircumcision, barbarian, Scythian, slave, free man, but Christ is all and in all* (Col. 3: 9 - 11).

Paul makes a statement here which is absolutely shocking. He says that you have *already* put off the old man and put on the new man. This is past tense. It has already been done. In fact, everything in this passage is written in the past tense except one part.

> *"...which is being renewed unto full knowledge..."*

What is being renewed unto full knowledge? The new man. But who is this new man? Verse eleven tells us that inside the new man there is only room for one person, Christ. Christ himself is the only content of this new man. But remember, you and I are *one* with him. So this Christ is a corporate Christ who is made up of many members (parts). He is both divinity and humanity.

So why would Christ need to be renewed? Because he is a Christ who is expressed through a corporate body. The body is made up of humans who have God living in them. But for those humans to be able to express the fullness of Christ, they must grow up into every aspect of him (Eph. 4:13-15).

The practical expression of him takes place as we allow him to renew our minds. The new man is already here. We need to see that and believe that. We need a whole new mindset. This happens as we shed the skin of the old man and allow the new man who is within to come forth. This takes place as we focus our minds and hearts on Christ (2 Cor. 3:18). [1]

However, please stand up and take notice. You, as an individual, are not the new man! The new man is the corporate Christ, the Head *and* the body, the Vine *and* the branches, the Bridegroom *and* the bride. Paul did not point out individual saints in the church in Colossae and tell them that they had put on the new man. No! He said that you (plural) have put on the new man. You see, at the end of this passage Paul tells us that the new man is Christ as the all *in all.* He was telling the church in Colossae that the new man is the Christ who is in all of them together.

This "new man" is your true identity. Dear believer, your true identity is not found in you yourself as a lone individual. It is not found in the individual Christian life. It is only found in the community life of the saints. It is only found in "together."

Now, I realize that what you just read may not sink in very far initially. You must realize that this renewing of the mind takes time. Your mind has already been preprogrammed to think on an individualistic basis only. This is dictated by many factors, the main ones being your culture, your background, and your education. The western culture is individualistic, plain and simple. It's very difficult for us to think in any other way. Our culture is becoming more and more individualistic every day.

Yet God's nature, life, and plan are all corporate. God himself is community. His purpose is all about community. The Bible, from cover to cover, is all about community. It is all about God's eternal plan to have a community of humans

---

[1]   See the author's book *The Temple Within.*

who contain his life and express his nature. Our God is triune: Father, Son, and Holy Spirit. It only makes sense, therefore, that his image (Christ) would also be corporate in nature and function.[2]

The old humanity (in Adam) was to be in his image (Christ). But that humanity fell and a new humanity was needed. This new humanity is the "new man" that Paul speaks of in Colossians and Ephesians. It is the corporate Christ made up of head and body.

The Growth of a Butterfly

Just as in every other area, we have relegated the area of Christian growth to be in the life of the individual. But actually, the butterfly grows *inside* the cocoon. Growth takes place inside the environment of body life, the life of the organic church. This has always been meant to be a process that takes place in the natural life of the believing community. Cocoon life means that you are growing into Christ *together* with your brothers and sisters.

> *And not holding the head, out from whom all the body, being richly supplied and knit together by means of the joints and sinews, grows with the growth of God (Col. 2:19).*

> *But holding to truth in love, we may grow up into him in all things, who is the head, Christ, out from whom all the body, being joined*

---

[2]   See the author's book *The Community Life of God*

> *together and being knit together through every joint of the rich supply and through the operation in the measure of each one part, causes the growth of the body unto the building up of itself in love* (Eph. 4:15, 16).

Please notice with me here that these two complementary passages say two different things about the direction of growth. In Colossians, the body grows *out from* the head. In Ephesians, the body grows *into* the head. Do you see that the head is the center of everything? Life and growth flow in and out of the head.

When the caterpillar is ready to pupate, he finds a branch, climbs on, attaches his back legs to the branch and then hangs upside down. Then he does something really interesting. He curls his head up to form a letter "J." His body is hanging down but his head is reaching upward. This is because all life flows from the head. The head supplies all nutrients needed to all of the body.

You are an important part of the body of Christ. All of your life comes from the Head, your Lord. All growth takes place in the body (cocoon). You cannot detach yourself from the body any more than a branch can detach itself from the tree. You are a member of Christ. This is who you are.

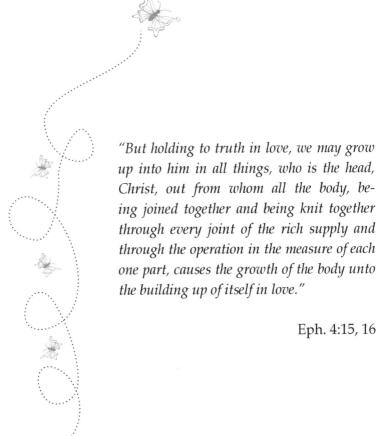

"But holding to truth in love, we may grow up into him in all things, who is the head, Christ, out from whom all the body, being joined together and being knit together through every joint of the rich supply and through the operation in the measure of each one part, causes the growth of the body unto the building up of itself in love."

Eph. 4:15, 16

Cocoon Cuisine

Remember our little friend, Fred? His main concern in life was to find the next weed patch with which to feed himself. He would search high and low to find the best foliage for the most delectable dinner possible. We are, after all, talking about weeds here!

Here is a picture of the individual Christian concerned with his own individual growth in his own individual walk with the Lord. He is constantly searching for more "food," so he is constantly searching for new "weed patches." Every Sunday morning he visits the "weed patch" to see if he can be "fed" for the week. All he is really concerned about is his own individual growth and well-being. He is forever being fed but never feeding. He is forever receiving but never giving. All of his food is taken externally. All of his food is taken individually. This is the life of the individual caterpillar.

However...

This is *not* the life inside the cocoon.

Life inside the cocoon is not about your obsession with your own individual walk with the Lord. It is no longer about your self-absorption, self-centeredness, and self-analysis. Please don't misunderstand me. I am *not* saying here that it is no longer about you. It *is* about you. But not the old you. The new you. The *real* you.

This real you is a part of a larger entity. The new you is an integral part of a larger living organism referred to as the body of Christ, the New Man, the Living Temple, the Bride of Christ, and the Family of God. Your true identity as an individual can only be found in relationship to this larger community of God. You can never be complete apart from this relationship.

> *And he put all things in subjection under his feet, and gave him as head over all things to the church, which is his body, the fullness of him who fills all in all* (Eph. 1: 22, 23).

You are still a wonderful individual! You are a saint (holy one) who was chosen before creation to be blameless before him. As wonderful as that is, it is still only *part* of the story. You are an integral part of a greater and even more wonderful Person.

That Person is Christ.

Jesus is the head and all of his "holy ones" are the body. What a magnificent Person this is. He is the fulfillment and realization of all of God's dreams. He is the center of all the universe. All things revolve around him. He is the full expression of the life of the Triune God. Life in him is community, love, peace, and joy.

But he has not been fully revealed yet. That's the purpose of the cocoon. It's within the life of community that the body is knit together and grows up in every aspect into the Head. This must become very practical. This must become our daily bread.

What's on the Menu?

In the cocoon life there is only one thing on the menu: Christ. Receiving Christ from your brothers and sisters. This involves receiving each one of them as members of Christ and receiving what they bring out from their own experiences of Christ. Only he is our true food and true drink (John 6:35). But that food and drink is given through the members of the body.

The food that is given is exactly what is needed for the transformation to take place. The food is *not* Bible studies and sermons. The food and drink is the living Person of Christ as he is experienced in the lives of his saints. These saints learn to fellowship with the true Bread of Life each day. Then, when they all come together, they open their mouths and share that Bread with one another. In other words, they break Bread together. The "Bread" is Christ as experienced by each one of them.

Now we know that in the natural world a caterpillar enters into the cocoon and a butterfly comes out. But this is only a picture. And every picture has limitations. In the real (spiritual) world, many caterpillars enter the cocoon but only one glorious butterfly comes out. We all enter into body life as isolated, individual believers. But something happens inside the cocoon. The metamorphosis that takes place inside is from the individualistic to the corporate. It's a radical change from the independent, self-serving life to the interdependent, community life. Self-sufficiency is not hailed as the ultimate goal in life inside the cocoon. Being a "self-made man" will not work in this environment. The old individualistic self must die and the new, corporate (community) self must emerge. But how does this transformation take place? Let's look to our cocoon for the answer.

It's All in the Soup

When the caterpillar enters into the cocoon a process begins which is altogether fascinating. The first thing that happens is that most of the caterpillar's old body dies. The same digestive juices that the caterpillar used in its old life to digest its food is now applied to its own body. You could say that the caterpillar digests itself from the inside out. This process is called "histolysis." The digestive juices make a sort of "soup" made of the old larval body.

However, not all of the insect's body is destroyed because there are some special cells which have remained hidden and have had no part to play in the old life. But now these "new life cells" become activated and get to work building a new body out of the "death soup" of the digestive juices. Life out of death. Does this sound familiar to you?

The Process of Death and Life

This is a picture of the transformation process that takes place inside the "cocoon" life of the body of Christ. The "new cells" of corporate life are hidden inside each believer. They are awakened and activated by the presence of the "death soup." But what is this death soup? It is nothing less than the death of Jesus Christ which is present in each one of us.

> For we who are alive are always being delivered unto death for Jesus' sake that the life of Jesus also may be manifested in our mortal flesh. So then death operates in us, but life in you (2 Cor. 4: 11, 12).

> ...that I may know him and the power of his resurrection and the fellowship of his sufferings, being conformed to his death; in order

*that I may attain to the resurrection from the
dead* (Phil. 3: 10, 11).

There is both the power of death *and* resurrection
working inside of you right now. Remember I said that
when you first turned to the Lord, the Father placed his
Seed within you? This Seed is Christ (the Son) himself and
this Seed contains all the life experience of the Son of God.
Part of this experience is death and resurrection.

Now when you are placed into the environment of
a close-knit community of believers (cocoon life), the *death
experience* of Christ in you becomes activated. The "digestive" juices come alive inside of you for the purpose of putting to death the old larval body.

But what is this old larva? It is your old life of isolation and individualism. It is your old mindset of being
an island to yourself. It is the old concepts that you, God,
and everyone else are just separated particles of individual
dust floating around in some kind of cosmic soup bowl. It
is not only the mindset but also the corresponding lifestyle
of the false self. The lifestyle that lives like you are an independent, self-governing, self-sufficient, self-centered, self-
absorbed, and self-realizing individual. This false self must
be consumed into the death of the Lord Jesus Christ.

He (the corporate Christ) must increase, but you (the
individual self) must decrease.

Of course, God does not want to do away with your
true self. This is the real you. This is your true identity
which I have been describing in this book. But you must
realize that the real you is not an isolated individual. You
are a part of the body of Christ. And that needs to become
extremely practical.

So we see that our food and drink inside the cocoon is Jesus Christ, including his death and resurrection. And this includes the corporate experience.

"We know love by this, that he laid down his life for us; and we ought to lay down our lives for the brethren."

1 John 3:16

Practical Community

Where does this idea of laying down one's life for another come from? Certainly John did not make this up out of thin air.

> *This is my commandment, that you love one another, just as I have loved you. Greater love has no one than this, that one lay down his life for his friends* (John 15: 12, 13).

Of course, we know that Jesus spoke these words to the twelve disciples. But where did Jesus get these ideas? Naturally, your first response would be to say that they came from God or from the Father. And this would be correct.

Now let me ask another question. *How* did these concepts come to Jesus? Did the Father set up a classroom and teach Jesus about love? No! Jesus brought these words out from his own experience with the Father. He has been loving the Father for a long time. And this love *is* the Holy Spirit.

But how was this divine love generated? It was generated by the Father laying down his life for the Son and the Son laying down his life for the Father.

You see, the Son already knew how to love because of all his experience in loving his Father throughout eternity. He already had plenty of experience in laying down his life for another. In fact, this was physically demonstrated by the Son on the Cross of Calvary. This is the actual lifestyle of God. He *is* eternal community. The lifeblood of that community is love. And love is the laying down of one's life for another. The Father is continually pouring out his life to the Son. The Son is continually pouring back that life to the Father. This love poured out is the Holy Spirit. [3]

> *The grace of the Lord Jesus Christ, and the love of God, and the fellowship of the Holy Spirit, be with you all* (2 Cor. 13:14).

This fellowship of the Godhead is throughout all the Scriptures. It is the foundation and the headwaters and the core life of the church. In reality, the community of the saints is to be a visible expression of the community life happening right now inside of God. This life together is what transforms us into the visible manifestation of the new creation. And all of this gets extremely practical.

My wife and I have been involved with several small groups of believers that I would call organic churches. They are *organic* because they live and function on the life of Jesus Christ within us. These groups usually all gather together once a week; the brothers get together at times and the sisters get together at other times. When we come together, all the saints are free to share Christ with one another in freedom under the direction of the Holy Spirit. We really cherish these times together because Jesus Christ is lifted up and the body is edified (or built up).

However, we are discovering that our identity together is not solely based upon our gatherings or scheduled meetings, as wonderful as they may be. We are not to be defined as a "meeting" or "gathering." We are not an

---

[3] See the author's book *The Community Life of God.*

event. We are an expression of the living, breathing body of Christ. Jesus Christ lives in us by his Spirit. He lives in us as individuals and he lives in us as a corporate entity. This cannot be limited to a meeting.

Therefore, the life within us must flow to all the members in a practical way at all times. This life can best be described by the English word "community." Yes, this life will be expressed within our gatherings, but it must flow outside our meetings as well. This is a *daily* life together and the expression must flow through reality.

The reality is the fact that we are the community of God. This is an already established fact. We are community because God is community. This corporate life exists inside each one of us. The community of the Father, Son, and Spirit lives inside you and me right now. But the problem is that this spiritual reality doesn't normally get to be expressed in a visible way. God's goal is that unseen realms would be brought into the seen realm. That his will would be done "on earth as it is in heaven." That his kingdom would break into our present, visible reality. This is where the laying down of our own lives comes into play.

I cannot express the community life of God unless I am willing to lay down my own life for my brothers and sisters. This is what we are all learning to do. Each one of us is endeavoring to break out of our own individual shell and join the rest in a "corporate cocoon." We have found that there are several "keys" to living this kind of life.

Communication

Setting up lines of communication is extremely important. If my brother or sister has a need, how will I ever know it if I don't keep "in touch"? We need to be sharing our lives with one another in an intimate way in order for us to care for one another. But this cannot happen without communication. Thank God for the telephone.

Years ago, there was a marketing slogan that the telephone company used.

"Reach out and touch someone."

This has become a slogan for us as well. We realize that every single day we need to touch and be touched by someone in Christ's body. So we all agreed that when any of us is thinking about another saint, that we don't let it stop there. We call them! It is so easy nowadays with cordless phones, cell phones, PDA's, and email to make contact with someone each day. Let's use these things for his glory.

Of course, there are other forms of communication besides the telephone. What about written communication? What about writing one another notes and cards? What about delivering a singing "telegram"? Several saints could get together, show up at another brother's or sister's house, ring the doorbell and sing. We can become very creative with our modes of communication. Just calling a saint to tell them you love them can make all the difference in their day.

Visiting One Another

This is in addition to scheduled gatherings. Inviting others over for dinner, or dessert, or a movie is very important. Then there is always the "drop by." Dropping in on other believers unexpectedly is also very important.

Doing Things Together

There are chores and errands that we all need to run on a constant basis. When I need to run to the bank, why not pick up another brother to hang out with on the way? The area that we live in here is very rural so we must drive longer distances to reach the grocery store, the mall, etc. Why not pick up others on the way? It's another opportunity to share our lives with one another.

Hindrances to Community

All of the activities I have been describing sound very wonderful. However, it must be understood that they are incredibly difficult to do. Why? Because of several hindrances or hurdles that stand in our way.

Our Individualistic Mindset

The first hindrance is the way we think about ourselves and our world. This mindset is the result of one event and an ongoing activity. The one-time event was the fall of man. The ongoing activity is the deceptive influence of the fallen angel.

We must remember that Satan was the first to break community with God. He is the original individualist. He stepped out of order and out of line to attempt to rise above the throne of God (Isa. 14:13). He separated himself because he wanted to be like God. Yet this was something that was reserved for another: the bride of Christ. An isolated individual angel or human could never be like God. That could only happen with a body (Eph. 1:22, 23).

Yet this is what the evil one used to tempt an individual in the garden. "You can be like God." But Eve (as an individual) could never be like God. That's because God is community and only a community could be "like him" (Gen. 1:26, 27).

And so ever since the fall, our minds have been "stuck" on an individualistic track. We relate to everything individualistically. We think that God is an individual, like us. We even read the Bible through individualistic colored "glasses." Even though most of the New Testament was written to a corporate entity called "the church," we still take those verses and see them as written to us as individuals. We cannot clearly see the New Testament because we cannot relate to the *context* in which it was written. It was written to communities of believers, not to individuals. But we cannot relate because most of us do not live in such community. So instead, we use our present culture as our vehicle to relate to the first century believers.

Our Present Culture

This is a major hurdle for us to overcome in order to live in true community. In case you haven't noticed, our western culture has become extremely busy, especially in the last fifty years or so. It seems that almost everything in our society is now about the individual and his rights, feelings, dreams, and self-acceptance, self-love, and self-esteem.

You, as an individual, coming to love and accept yourself is the key to everything, the psychologists tell us. Yet this is exactly the opposite of what the Lord Jesus told us.

He told us to deny ourselves and lose our own lives (Matt. 16:24-26). In fact, he commended leaving everything to follow him (Matt. 19:29). This was not just to follow some cause or political activity. This was to follow him. To do his Father's will which is to build an eternal community of family that would live in oneness with the Triune God (Matt. 12: 46-50). In other words, he was saying to leave the self-centered lifestyle of your own culture and society. We are to be different. We are to be a loving community under the direct headship of Jesus Christ.

Yet we still live in this individualistic culture. Even the Eastern cultures are becoming individualized because of the Western influence. Our best defense in fighting this influence is by building strong community with our brothers and sisters in Christ. This all begins with a deep revelation of our oneness in him.

"The new man is there set forth as the church, the body of Christ, and this new man is to grow unto the measure of the stature of the fullness of Christ. It is the corporate man that grows to that stature; individuals cannot do so. Only in relatedness do we move into the fullness of Christ...

It is the setting aside of everything individual, personal, separate, as such, and putting on that consciousness of relationship in which everything is for the body, and in the body, and by the body. It is by this fellowship of spirit that the Lord gains his end and we come to the Lord's end."

T. Austin-Sparks
The Stewardship of the Mystery

The Whole Christ

There is a song that we sometimes sing with the saints.

"King Jesus is our head,
The rest of him are we.
His body and his bride His ancient mystery.
He raised us from the dead
And filled us with his life
He's coming back again
To claim his holy wife."

This song does a good job of describing another, and most vital, aspect of our true identity: our oneness with Christ.

Oneness is something that the natural mind will never comprehend. How can the Triune God be three Persons who are one God? The natural mind cannot grasp such a thing. Therefore, this idea of oneness can only be apprehended in spirit. Your spirit already understands oneness because that is the very nature of spirit. The flesh does not understand because the flesh is all about separateness and isolation.

Oneness and Spirit

Let me give you an illustration of how oneness works. It only truly works in spirit. Let's say that you live near a body of water. Let's say that this body of water is a lake. The water in this lake represents spirit. Now, you go home and grab a large empty bucket and take it down to the lake. You walk into the lake with the bucket and begin pushing the bucket into the water. What will happen? The bucket will fill with water, of course. Now, let go of the bucket. What happens? The bucket sinks down to the bottom of the lake. This happens because the bucket is now filled with water. The bucket is "one" with the lake. Why? Because the water is *in* the bucket and the bucket is *in* the water. Remember, the water is representing spirit here. Does this help you to understand how you are one with Christ?

It is because Christ (Spirit) lives in you, and you live in Christ (Spirit). Therefore you are *one* with him! This means that you share his nature and life, but not his deity. He alone is God. But we are partakers of the divine nature (2 Pet. 1:4) and his life (1 John 5:12). We have been submerged into his Spirit and that Spirit has filled us to overflowing. Therefore, dear saint, you are one with your Lord (1 Cor. 6:17)! This is all made possible by something called "spirit."

Head and Body - the One New Man

But you are not alone. Many other people are also one with him. Every true (Spirit-born) believer is one with Christ. So we are all in the lake together! This makes us one with him and one with each other.

> *For even as the body is one and has many members, yet all the members of the body, being many, are one body, so also is the Christ* (1 Cor. 12:12).

If you read this verse carefully, you will see that Paul is saying that the body, the church, is Christ. We all know that the head is Christ, but here Paul states that the body is *also* Christ. How can this be? It's actually very simple when you consider oneness.

All the members of the body (you and I) are "in Christ." Is this not true? And is it not also true that all the members of the body have Christ in them? Christ in us, and us in Christ. This means we are one with the head, who is Christ. The head and the body are one! Of course, this only stands to reason. Who ever heard of a headless body or a bodiless head? A *whole* person is made up of *both* head and body. And so it is with Christ. He is, of course, a whole and complete Person. The whole Christ is made up of *both* head and body.

But why have we (in our minds) chopped off his head and separated it from his body? Why do we think of Christ as being divided? Why can't we wrap our minds around the oneness of Christ? It is because of the fall. When Adam fell we inherited a fallen mind which divides and separates everything. It is very difficult for us to think in terms of wholeness and oneness. Our minds want to dissect and separate everything into neat little categories and compartments. Oneness just doesn't fit into that agenda.

Yet the truth of the oneness of the head and the body stands. And we can only receive it by a revelation of the Holy Spirit. This revelation was given to Paul in a special way. And he referred to this oneness of the head and body as the One New Man (Eph. 2:11-18; Eph. 4:11-13, 20-24; Col. 3:9-11).

> *And have put on the new man, which is being renewed unto full knowledge according to the*

> *image of him who created him, where there can-*
> *not be Greek and Jew, circumcision and uncir-*
> *cumcision, barbarian, Scythian, slave, free man,*
> *but Christ is all and in all* (Col. 3:10, 11).

Paul tells us that this New Man needs to be "put on" like a garment (Eph. 4:24), and that this happens by the renewing of our minds (Rom. 12:2). We need to "put on" the mind of the New Man. This is a corporate mind. This is a mind of oneness. The oneness of the head and body. The oneness of Christ.

This New Man is not an individual entity. He is a corporate Man made up of many members. This Man is being renewed day by day by the minds of the members being conformed to the one mind of the head. The content of this New Man is Christ. He is all and in all. There are no distinctions of race, color, nationality, class, gender, or station in life. Christ is all!

The New Man Consciousness

It is in this body life (or cocoon life) that we put on the New Man and grow together into the measure of the stature of the fullness of Christ (Eph. 4:13). This is the environment where we discover our true identity. I have written this book to help you see who you are in Christ. But please understand that you can never fully discover who you are without cocoon life. It's only in corporate living that you will discover your true individuality. Isn't that a paradox? It only *seems* logical that I would discover my uniqueness by isolating myself into a shell of "selfrealization." But that is not the way at all. It is only by being closely knit together with other brothers and sisters that I can see the *contrast;* and my own uniqueness as a part of the body comes alive. I can see who I am by seeing who my brothers and sisters are. Not only that, but they can see who I am as well. We can discover who we are together, not in the flesh, but in Christ (2 Cor. 5:16). But this can only happen as we develop a consciousness of the *whole* Christ.

Each one of us, as individuals, must allow God to renew our minds so that we no longer think as separate individuals. This is part of "putting on the new man." We must put on the consciousness or awareness of the New Man. This must become our awareness twenty-four hours per day. This is something that we can help one another develop on a daily basis.

To learn to think corporately requires a revelation of the wholeness of Christ. This is the oneness of the head and body. This revelation is the beginning. Then, from there, you must move on to develop a new mindset - a corporate mindset. This paradigm is completely new for us. You and I do not normally think in terms of "us" and "we." It's all about "I" and "me." But that mindset must shift to the community mindset and that takes time.

You and I will never fully comprehend our true identities unless we can see the New Man. We are members of the body of Christ. This makes us members of Christ (1 Cor. 6:15). Is not the body part of Christ? The head is Christ *and* the body is Christ. This is the New Man, where Christ is all and in all.

This is your identity. You are a part of the living Christ. You are one with him and you are one with the other parts, your brothers and sisters. Nothing can separate you from the One New Man (Rom. 8: 37-39). Your oneness with him is based upon the stability of his oneness with his Father (John 17:22). This oneness is secure and will last throughout eternity. This oneness is not based upon what you do or say. It is not based upon your successes or failures. It is based upon *his* victory on the cross!

The one grain of wheat became the many grains (John 12:24). Jesus Christ was increased (John 3:30). Jesus Christ was enlarged and many were added to him. He is being glorified.

And you are part of him!

"When we touch the genuine church life we may feel somewhat uncomfortable. This is because the undealt-with self does not fit in the church. In my own experience, when I first touched the church life I felt exposed. My natural life and self was laid bare for what it was. The light shining in all the saints made me realize that my seminary experience did not matter here. What I thought I knew did not matter. Reputation or eloquence did not count. What mattered was Christ!"

Bill Freeman
Seeing and Feeling the Church

The Pool of Death

*And Jesus answered them, saying, 'The hour
has come for the Son of Man to be glorified.
Truly, truly, I say to you, unless the grain of
wheat falls into the ground and dies, it abides
alone; but if it dies, it bears much fruit. He
who loves his soul-life loses it; and he who
hates his soul-life in this world shall keep it
unto eternal life'* (John 12: 23-25).

Jesus Christ was glorified by increasing. The one grain of
wheat died in order to produce the many grains. The
Lord was glorified by becoming bigger. The one man, Jesus, was multiplied to produce the corporate man, Christ.
This corporate man is the One New Man I spoke of in the
last chapter, who is made up of many members. You and I
are part of him.

But this could only take place through death. The resurrection produced the many grains. But before that could
happen, there had to be a death. The grain of wheat had
to fall into the ground. Now we all know that Jesus Christ
died on the cross and rose from the dead to produce the
church and that is a wonderful thing. But what does that
have to do with you and me, practically speaking, right
here and now?

The Loss of Life

It has everything to do with you and me right here and now and that's because of verse twenty-five.

> *"He who loves his soul-life loses it; and he who hates his soul-life in this world shall keep it unto life eternal."*

This becomes very practical in two ways: the individual and the relational.

Your Individual Life - Christ as the Preeminent One

> *And he is the head of the body, the church; he is the beginning, the firstborn from the dead, that he himself might have the first place in all things* (Col. 1:18).

The first place of death is in your own personal life. Does Christ have the preeminence? Does he have the first place *in all things?* Before there can be true community life, there must be a death that happens in each individual life. The caterpillar goes into the cocoon for the purpose of dying to himself. The digestive juices are now used to actually digest the caterpillar itself. The caterpillar lays down his own interests and his own life so that the butterfly can come forth.

Each area of the life of the individual believer must be dealt with. Family, career, friends, money, hobbies, sports, leisure, business, and all personal passions must be plunged into this pool of death. Does Christ, the whole Christ (head and body), have the first place *in all things* in each of our lives?

We are learning to lay down our own personal interests and dreams for the eternal purpose of God. This is not easy. Our culture is so self-absorbed and self-centered that we have actually come to believe that this way of life is normal. But our only common interest need be Christ himself.

This is the Christ-life. This is the corporate life. This is community life. He becomes our All when we lay everything down at his feet. Material possessions become as nothing when we realize that the only precious commodity that we have is our brothers and sisters in Christ. When this reality becomes our awareness, then we can't wait to see our brothers and sisters again. We will go out of our way to see them. We will make excuses to see them. But it requires me to lay down my own personal life for this to happen.

My life will always butt heads with Christ's life. And what is his life? His life is the community life. His life is a life of oneness with his Father in the Spirit. His life is the corporate life of continually laying down and giving up his own life. But his life interrupts my own life. His life "interferes" with my own life. In fact, his life demands that I lay down my own personal life. I cannot live the community life with my brothers and sisters if I insist on retaining my own life. If Christ becomes the preeminent one in my life, then that means the "Christ-lifestyle" will become preeminent as well. The Christ-life is a life of oneness.

A Man after God's Own Heart

Why was David referred to as a "man after God's own heart"? It was simply because David laid down all of his own personal interests for the sake of God's own desire and satisfaction.

> *Remember, O Lord, on David's behalf, all his affliction; how he swore to the Lord and vowed to the mighty One of Jacob, 'Surely I will not enter my house, nor lie on my bed; I will not give sleep to my eyes or slumber to my eyelids, until I find a place for the Lord, a dwelling place for the Mighty One of Jacob'* (Ps. 132: 1-5)

David was willing to give up all that was *his* so that God could get what he wanted: a house. Are you willing to lay down your own life so that God can have his own house, family, image, body, and bride? The butterfly will never fly free until the caterpillar willingly lays down his own life. Personal death brings forth corporate resurrection life.

Christ Our Life

It seems to me that many Christians today are seeking after their own personal health, wealth, and happiness. They are actively seeking for the "secret formula" that will teach them how to think the right thoughts and say the right words to give them personal success in some area. That is the direct opposite of what Jesus Christ told us. He told us to lose our lives, not to try to make them successful. A successful caterpillar is still just a caterpillar! He will only become a butterfly by losing his "caterpillar life." That happens in the "pool of death" which is located inside the cocoon. The progression of death to life begins with you first being in the right environment, community life with brothers and sisters. From there, it moves on to you (personally) laying down your own life for Christ and his church. Then it proceeds to your relationship with the saints.

The death is a daily laying down of our lives for the brethren (1 John 3:16). You can't do that, however, if you are entangled with the affairs of this life. There just won't be enough time. If Christ is not your All, if he is not the Center and the Head, and if he does not have the preeminence, then there won't be enough time for the saints. Simply put, you will be *too busy* with family, friends, jobs, recreation, etc., to lay your life down for the brethren. This shows that you have not yet lost your own soul-life. You are still hanging onto it because you believe *that* is who you are. But that life is *not* who you are at all.

> *Set your mind on the things which are above, not on the things which are on the earth. For you died and your life is hidden with Christ in God. When Christ our life is manifested, then you also will be manifested with him in glory* (Col. 3:2-4).

Why does the Lord Jesus call you to lose your soul-life? It's because that life is dead! The only life you have is hidden with Christ in God. Paul tells us that now, "Christ is *our* life." Did you notice that he switched from the singular to the plural? Christ is *our* life. Christ is not a singular life. Christ is the plural life, the community life. He is *our* life together. And the only thing that can stand in the way of that life is your old, dead soul-life. This is no longer your identity. Now, your only life, your only identity, is Christ (who is *our* life).

Does this mean that you can't have a family, or career, or friends? Of course not! But it does mean that none of those things are primary. Christ now has the first place in all these things. All of those things are related to the pre-eminent Christ, the whole Christ who is head and body. This is true because it is *this* Christ who is *our* life.

It is in the fires of true church life that you will have the opportunity to lay down your own soul-life and pick up his divine life. This happens as you lay down that soul-life for your brothers and sisters. It is when you lay down your own desires and interests and become sensitive to the needs of the saints. It is when you esteem your brother more highly than yourself. It is when you develop a "body consciousness" and begin to live the body life that your own soul-life, that dead thing, begins to fall away.

And when this happens, the living Christ can be seen again!

"But you did not so learn Christ, if indeed you have heard him and have been taught in him as the reality is in Jesus, that you put off, as regards your former manner of life, the old man, which is being corrupted according to the lusts of the deceit, and that you be renewed in the spirit of your mind and put on the new man, which was created according to God in righteousness and holiness of the reality."

Eph. 4:20-24

Learning Christ

We are learning that genuine church life or body life is the proper environment for the metamorphosis of caterpillar into butterfly. This means the transformation from the individual Christian life into the community life of the body. This is the life of oneness, the oneness of the head and the body, Christ and the church.

This takes time because our minds need to be renewed from individualistic thinking to corporate thinking. Our identities as individuals are intricately tied to our relationships with our brothers and sisters. What I am saying is that you will never fully discover your true identity and purpose apart from being woven into a close-knit group of believers. That is the path to discovery of identity. That is the way to revelation of purpose. And that is also the route to awareness of practical wisdom and knowledge.

Our Method of Learning

We learn how to live by watching the Corporate Christ. We really don't know how to be ourselves until we see our identity in context, that is, our identity "in Christ."

> *That their hearts may be comforted, they being knit together in love and unto all the riches of the full assurance of understanding, unto the full knowledge of the mystery of God, Christ. In whom all the treasures of wisdom and knowledge are hidden* (Col 2:2, 3).

There is a great emphasis these days, among Christians, to learn about God and to learn the Bible. I have heard many Christians say that we must learn the "Word of God" and I couldn't agree more. The problem comes in with a misunderstanding about what the "Word of God" is. Most Christians will tell you that the "Word" is the Bible. So we must all learn the Bible.

Now, please do not misunderstand me. I am all for knowing and studying the Scriptures. That should be very apparent to you in the course of reading this book. But I believe that the popular definition of the "Word of God" falls extremely short of what the Scriptures themselves teach. Here again, because of our fallen minds, we like to take things pertaining to God and split them and dissect them like a laboratory frog. The Scriptures are only a small part of the wholeness which is the Word of God.

Actually, according to the Scriptures themselves, the Word of God is a Person.

> *And the Word became flesh and tabernacled among us and we beheld his glory, glory as of the only begotten from the Father, full of grace and truth* (John 1:14).

> *And he is clothed with a garment dipped in blood; and his name is called the Word of God* (Rev. 19:13).

Obviously, the Word of God is the Son of God. This Word became flesh in the man Jesus Christ. The Scriptures are the written revelation of the mind, thought, and purpose of God. So these scriptures are God-breathed and

God-inspired and are therefore the Word of God to us. But the living God can only be fully expressed through a Person, that is, Christ. He is the Word of God. He is the full image, expression, and embodiment of the living God. And this expression can only be fully realized through the *whole* Christ, the corporate Christ (Eph. 1:22, 23).

But you did not so learn Christ... (Eph. 4:20).

So learning the Word of God means to learn Christ. This is all about learning a Person and that Person is a community made up of head and body.

This opens up the gateway to a whole new "method" of learning. No longer are we sitting in a "classroom" listening to a lecture being given by a "teacher." We are no longer students in that sense, but we are now members of a living Person. That Person is made up of many members and as we relate to those "members" we relate to that Person. We learn this Person by relating to all of his parts. We learn all about Life from this corporate/community Person. In fact, we learn how to be an individual by living in this Person.

Even natural, biological life tells us this. When you were born, physically, you were born into a family. It's within the community life of the family that you learn to be an individual. If, for some reason, that family life is denied you, your individuality will not develop properly. Your own personality and growth potential will be stunted. Your own identity and personality development depend upon having the proper environment which is community life. This is a picture of Christ and the church.

Learning Our Identity

One of the first things you must learn is your true identity in Christ. You cannot learn this just by reading this book! This book can help point the way but your identity is found "in Christ." Your identity is found in a Person. It is only as you live in this Person that you discover who you are.

This "learning" begins with a revelation from the Father through the Spirit to your spirit. However, seeing that you are an integral part of the body of Christ universally is not enough. You must also be a functioning part of a close-knit group of believers locally.

In a group of believers where grace, freedom, and acceptance flow, you are released to truly discover who you are in Christ. I don't have to prove anything to the saints because they accept me for who I am and that allows me to relax and accept them as well. The struggle comes into play with no longer knowing each other after the flesh, but instead knowing one another according to the new creation. I am learning to relate to them in a completely new way. I am learning to see them "in Christ" as the new creation. This reveals to me their true identities and I can then describe to them what I see. I see them as they truly are: holy ones inside of Jesus Christ. Now, I can declare to them who they really are. And, of course, they can tell me who I am in Christ also.

Of course, this "seeing" my brothers and sisters for who they really are must not end with me just making declarations to them. This revelation must progress onward to the point where I actually do something for them. Spending time together, eating together and taking care of one another is all part of this community life. This "cocoon life" is the environment in which you discover your true identity as an ongoing corporate experience with other saints.

Learning How to Live

As I have said before, this metamorphosis or transformation is all about moving from the isolated individual experience to the corporate-community experience. And this becomes very practical. It touches every area of daily life in a very intimate way. Of course, inside the "cocoon" things get really close and intimate. We are talking about practically expressing the real oneness that we have in Christ. But that oneness is just a nice idea or concept until it is "fleshed out" in the real lives of people. When you are part of a close-knit group of believers, this can actually happen.

We have always thought that we need to teach the church, and of course, this is true. God raises up people to equip the church (Eph. 4: 11, 12). However, have we ever considered that we could learn from the church? Can the church corporate teach the church individual? What I am asking is this: can the individuals within the church learn from the corporate body? Can I learn by observing the corporate Christ? As I watch the church deal with problems and situations, can I apply those solutions to my own life personally? I definitely believe so and have seen it happen. If all of the treasures of wisdom and knowledge are found in Christ (Col. 2:2-3), then doesn't it make sense that they will be found in his body as well? And these "treasures" can be found in the saints and applied to every area of life.

The real "teaching" we all need is not to be found in a classroom. It is found in the daily life of the body of Christ. I have personally learned a lot about unity by watching the brothers and sisters in the groups I have been in. We are developing relationships with other believers (and groups of believers) within our city. This is extremely important to us. We do not want to become an ingrown toenail in the body. We are learning to become open and inclusive rather than closed and exclusive.

Even though others may be different from us, if they have Jesus Christ living in them then they are our brothers and we receive them. This is a wonderful reality that God is showing us right now and he is teaching it to us by our seeing the body at work.

We have heard it said that it takes a village to raise a child. I believe that is true as long as the child is in the right village! The "village" or community must be the community of Jesus Christ and not the village of this world system. Many Christian parents have switched over to home schooling because they understand this. But why, oh why, can't the same parents see that the church must come home as well? We feel that we must remove our children from the educational system and yet we leave ourselves in the religious system.

In body life you will learn how to be a parent. You will learn this together with your brothers and sisters. You will learn that parenting, just like everything else, is a corporate experience and not just an individual one. You will learn to be a father by being part of a brotherhood where there are other fathers. You will learn to be a mother by being in a sisterhood where there are other mothers. You will all discover these things together.

This also applies to marriage, wives and husbands, employees, employers, students, children, and every other walk of life. Everything changes when it becomes a together thing. God never intended us all to be isolated units who "learn" and struggle on our own. He designed us to be corporate creatures who look to one another to discover our identities and learn how to live. Of course, our fallen minds resist this kind of lifestyle because of our "isolation syndrome." But divine life is waiting to be discovered by us in the midst of our brethren in Christ.

> *Behold, how good and how pleasant it is for the brothers to dwell together in unity. It is like the precious oil upon the head, coming down upon the beard, even Aaron's beard, coming down upon the edge of his robes. It is like the dew of Hermon coming down upon the mountains of Zion; for there the Lord commanded the blessing life forever* (Psalm 133).

PART THREE

The Butterfly

"For the anxious watching of the creation eagerly awaits the revelation of the sons of God. For the creation was made subject to vanity, not of its own will, but because of him who subjected it. In hope that the creation itself will also be freed from the slavery of corruption into the freedom of the glory of the children of God."

Rom. 8: 19-21

"And because you are sons, God has sent forth the Spirit of his Son into our hearts, crying, 'Abba! Father!'"

Gal. 4:6

Turning Inside Out

The discovery of your identity in Christ is, in reality, an endless journey. Since your identity is found in your oneness with him, this discovery is endless because he is endless. However, this journey does take us into progressively deeper phases of revelation and awareness. We have seen this using the illustration of the metamorphosis of the butterfly.

We know that the caterpillar himself was born containing the seed of the butterfly within him. What happens inside the cocoon is the metamorphosis or transformation of caterpillar into butterfly. But this happens as the old caterpillar dies and the butterfly from within is born. Now what is birth, essentially?

Well, we know that pregnancy is the conception and development of one person living inside of another. The unborn child grows and develops inside of the mother. You could say that the mother is the "carrier" for the new person until they are ready to come out into the world. It is the same way for the butterfly with one major exception. The caterpillar dies and the butterfly take his place. This is not *addition,* it is *replacement.* But the butterfly within does need to come out at some point in time. Now, here is my point. The transformation takes place by that which is within coming out. The internal becomes external. The caterpillar turns himself inside out.

This is the putting on of the New Man, who is Christ. This Christ, who is within you, is the hope of glory. But what is glory? It is the outward manifestation or expression of that which is within. Christ is that hope of glory. But it is Christ in a particular location: Christ *in* you. So what I am saying is that the glorification of God happens only when the Christ within you is revealed. He, who is within, must come out. All of the treasures of wisdom and knowledge are hidden inside of you (Col. 2:3). But these must come out for glorification to take place.

Putting on the New Man (Christ) is like saying: *pull from within those things that are Christ and bring them out.* We put on Christ like we put on a coat or other garment. But where do we get this garment? We take it out from the closet and the closet is our spirit. Your spirit is the repository for all the unsearchable riches of Christ. You need to reach down deep into the "closet" and pull out all of those beautiful garments. And then wear those garments in your daily life.

Your Kingdom Come

> *Your kingdom come, your will be done on earth as it is in heaven...* (Matt. 6:10).

Jesus told us to pray that God's kingdom would come to this earth. We know that his kingdom is from another realm. It is the kingdom "of heaven." It is the heavenly kingdom. It is the kingdom from "above." But where are the heavens? Where do the heavenly places reside? Paul tells us that the heavenlies reside within Christ (Eph. 1:3). And this Christ resides within you. This means that the heavenlies are inside of you. Don't you remember him saying that the kingdom of God is inside of you?

So the kingdom of God (heaven) must come to the earth. One realm must enter into another realm. The internal must enter the external. The unseen must enter the seen. In other words, Jesus Christ must be made visible. This happens as you and I take what is inside of us and bring it out. The Christ in us must be brought out and worn as a garment. This is done through both our words and actions, but these are always done through the flow of life, not through religion or human effort.

Man's Religion vs. Christ

We must realize that this "putting on" of Christ is totally done by grace and life and not in the power of our own flesh. It happens as we allow his Spirit to renew our minds and permeate our souls. This is not some adherence to an external code. This all happens *internally* by the life of Christ.

This was the error of the Galatians. They were trying to perfect in the flesh what God had begun in the Spirit (Gal. 3: 1-3). It is true that you and I must actually "put on" Christ, but even this is done *by* Christ, *in* Christ, and *for* Christ.

By turning ourselves inside out the glorious butterfly is released. The internal becomes external in Christ and he becomes our outer garment. This, of course, takes place both individually and corporately. But how can we walk in this experience in a practical way?

The Preeminence of Christ

> *He is also head of the body, the church; and he is the beginning, the firstborn from the dead, so that he himself will come to have first place in everything* (Col. 1:18).

Paul tells us that God's eternal purpose is to sum up or head up all things into Christ (Eph. 1: 9, 10). All things were at one time in him (Col. 1:16), but have now fallen out of him through the rebellion of Lucifer and the fall of man. God's purpose is to have all things reconciled to him that he would be the head, center, and life of all things (Col. 1:19, 20). The church (the corporate Christ) is the sphere in which the summing up or heading up of all things in Christ takes place. He must have the *first place* in all things. But how will this happen if we don't bring him into every situation?

Do you have a job? Are you a parent? Are you a spouse? Are you a student? I would propose to you that you are not any of these things, but rather, these are activities that you engage in. Your true identity has been presented to you in this book. Your true identity is a part of Jesus Christ. Your true identity is a part of the body of Christ. Now... how are you going to bring out the real you? How are you going to bring Christ into these activities that you are engaged in? How is he going to have the first place in all these things?

There are some friends of ours who really enjoy canning fruit. They are not "fruit canners," they just enjoy this activity. But how can they bring Christ into this activity? Well, the first thing that comes to mind is how they can "see" Christ in this endeavor. Fruit comes from a tree.

Fruit is the product of life. Fruit is also the seed of life. Of course, Jesus Christ is the True Vine (Tree of Life) and we are his branches (John 15). These sisters are taking Christ and storing him in their spirits so that they can distribute him to others at a later date. This is the heart of "fruit canning." They can discuss this as they are canning.

They can sing and share him with one another as they are canning. He can have the preeminence in fruit canning!

What about your activities and relationships? Can he have the first place in all of those as well? He can if you bring him into every situation. He can if you put on Christ in everyday life.

Let me ask you a question. Do you believe that Jesus Christ lives inside of you? If your answer is yes, then I would ask you to read the following statement out loud:

"I believe that Jesus Christ lives inside of me."

Now, based upon your confession of faith, when you wake up tomorrow morning what are you going to do with Jesus Christ? How are you going to touch him? How are you going to converse with him? How are you going to fellowship with him? Are you going to ignore him? Or, are you going to acknowledge and be aware of him throughout the day? Are you going to put him on as you put on your clothes?

Now... I have another question for you:

Do you believe that Jesus Christ lives in your brothers and sisters (fellow believers)?

If he lives in your brothers and sisters then how are you going to find him there today? What are you going to do with Jesus Christ in the saints today? How are you going to touch him in the saints today? How are you going to see their true identity today?

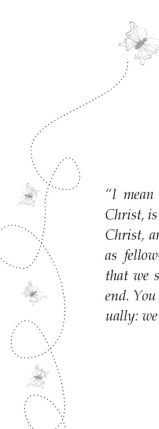

"I mean that sonship requires the body of Christ, is involved in that truth of the Body of Christ, and it is in our relatedness in Christ as fellow-heirs that we shall be developed, that we shall come to fullness, to God's full end. You and I cannot inherit singly, individually: we can only inherit in a related way."

T. Austin-Sparks
God's Spiritual House

Our Sonship in Christ

As we move along into the progression of God's purpose for us, we can't help but see that he is after a life that matures. As I pointed out in the first part of this book, the Father deposits his life into us by giving us his only begotten Son. This life is given as a seed. It is whole and complete and perfectly divine. However, it needs to mature. God is wanting us to grow up into him in all things.

> Out from whom all the body, being joined together and being knit together through every joint of the rich supply and through the operation in the measure of each one part, causes the growth of the body unto the building up of itself in love (Eph. 4:16).

If you are a believer, then you are a true child of God. But the Scriptures make it very clear that God wants his children to grow up into mature sons. You could say that God wants spiritual adults. You are a son, but God wants you to grow up into a mature son, an adult person. Now as we can see in this Scripture, this happens within the church, the body of Christ. We grow *together* through the rich supply and operation of each part. In other words, the body grows by each member contributing and functioning in and with their respective gifts and ministries. But let's first take a look at the meaning of sonship itself.

The Sonship of Jesus Christ

> *And behold a voice out of the heavens said,
> 'This is my beloved Son, in whom I am well
> pleased!'* (Matt. 3:17).

> *No one has ever seen God; the only begotten
> Son, who is in the bosom of the Father, he has
> declared him* (John 1:18).

Jesus Christ is the only begotten Son of God. The word "only" denotes that he is unique because he is the eternal Son of God, God himself. The word "begotten" does not mean that at some point he became the Son. He has always been the eternal Son. However, this term denotes the idea that he flows out from the Father. This is not an event, but rather, a continuous flowing of divine life. The Father pours out everything that he is into his Son. The Son perfectly declares or explains the Father. He is the perfect image or expression of the Father.

The Father takes all his delight in his Son. In fact, the Son is the only Person who can truly please the Father. All of the Father's attention is on the Son. It is the Father's goal to sum up all things in this universe into his Son (Eph. 1: 9, 10). In human terms, you could say that the Father is totally obsessed with his Son and that he only has eyes for his Son.

Jesus Christ made it very clear that he and the Father are one (John 17:21, 22). In fact, at one point, the Jews picked up rocks to stone him when he said this (John 10: 30, 31). This is because oneness is always misunderstood. It is always considered to be heresy. How could Jesus claim to be one with God? It's because he is in the Father and the

Father is in him. The Father and the Son are one and their relationship of love *is* the Holy Spirit.

Jesus Christ is the only begotten Son of God. He is the unique eternal Son of the Father. There can be no other like him. And yet, Paul tells us that he is the firstborn among many brethren (Rom. 8:29).

Many Sons in the One Son

Did you know that you are a son of the living God? In fact, I am going to really go out on a doctrinal limb here and make the follow statement:

> *You are as much a son of God as Jesus Christ!*

How can I make such a statement? It's actually very easy. There is only one Sonship. Have you ever wondered why the New Testament calls you a "son" of God regardless of your gender? Nowhere does it refer to women as the "daughters" of God. Does this mean that God is sexist? Of course not! It means that there is only *one* Sonship and that Sonship is the relationship between Jesus Christ and his Father. You are called a son because he is *the* Son. You are one with him, so you share in his Sonship with the Father. There is only *one* eternal Son. Yet within the one Son there are many sons. This is *the Sonship* of which the Scriptures speak.

There are two companion scriptures in the writings of Paul that make this very clear:

> *For as many as are led by the Spirit of God, these are sons of God. For you have not received a spirit of slavery bringing you into*

> *fear again, but you have received a spirit of*
> *sonship in which we cry, 'Abba! Father!'*
> (Rom. 8:14, 15).

And then...

> *That He might redeem those under the law*
> *that we might receive the sonship. And be-*
> *cause you are sons, God has sent forth the*
> *Spirit of his Son into our hearts crying,*
> *'Abba! Father!' So then you are no longer*
> *a slave but a son; and if a son, an heir also*
> *through God* (Gal. 4: 5-7)

I would like to point out two important points in these two passages. First, in Romans 8:15 who is doing the crying? Paul says it is *we* who cry 'Abba! Father!' And yet in Galatians, who is doing the crying?

In Galatians 4:6 it is the "Spirit of his Son" who does the crying. We cry and the Spirit cries because his Spirit has become one with our spirit (1 Cor. 6:17). It is actually one and the same crying. We cry because the one Son cries. And what do we cry? We cry a declaration of our intimacy with the Father. But how can we make such a bold declaration? We can make it because we are a part of the one Sonship of Jesus Christ.

And that brings me to my second point in these passages. In Galatians 4:5, we are told that we have received *the sonship.* It does not say that we have received many individual sonships. We all only receive one sonship and that is the sonship of the one Son, Jesus Christ. We are all sons because we are all in the one Son. I guess you could think of it this way. The Son is a huge ship. We are all passengers aboard that ship and that makes us sons as well. We are all cruising on-board the Son-ship.

This holds incredible implications for you and me.

Prayer

Have you ever wondered how the Lord Jesus could make such statements as, "Whatever you ask for in my name, the Father will give it to you"? The key here is the meaning of the phrase "in my name." What does it mean to ask in his name? It means to ask in the sonship. Because you and I are in the Son, we can ask the Father in the one sonship.

It is the spirit of sonship which cries out, "Abba! Father!" And it is that same spirit that lives in us and prays through us (Rom. 8:26, 27). This spirit knows the mind and will of God and prays accordingly. It is Christ (the Son) praying in you (a son). And even more powerfully, it is Christ (the Son) praying in us (the Corporate Son). That is why the Father will answer. It is his Son who is asking! The one in whom he is well-pleased.

Our Inheritance

> *The Spirit himself witnesses with our spirit that we are children of God. And if children, heirs also; on the one hand, heirs of God; on the other, joint heirs with Christ, if indeed we suffer with him that we may also be glorified with him* (Rom 8:16, 17).

In this passage, we can see the progression from children to mature sons. What makes the difference? It is suffering. You progress and mature from child to mature son through sufferings. It is through many tribulations that we enter into the kingdom of God. The suffering comes in the form of persecution and wrestling with the self-life or soul-life. Every day you have the opportunity to lose your life and gain his life.

But what is this wonderful inheritance? It is the Triune God himself. We have been given the Holy Spirit as a down payment or sample of the fullness of the Triune God. But there will come a time when you and I will enjoy the fullness of God. The Spirit is the guarantee of that future fullness.

> *In whom you also, having heard the word of the truth, the gospel of your salvation, in him also believing, you were sealed with the Holy Spirit of the promise, who is the pledge of our inheritance unto the redemption of the acquired possession, to the praise of his glory* (Eph. 1: 13, 14)

"This is not a situation where a few devout Christians occasionally come together to worship. This is the creation of a counter-community with a distinct social environment. As the disciples of Jesus come together, their agenda and corporate structure will appear upside down in contrast to conventional social organizations, including many churches."

Donald B. Kraybill
The Upside-Down Kingdom

The Kingdom

"These men who have upset the world have come here also..." (Acts 17:6b)

When the butterfly begins to emerge from the husk of the cocoon, life takes a radical turn. The butterfly no longer lives like a caterpillar. The differences between the two lifestyles are enormous.

Obviously, the butterfly looks completely different from the caterpillar. But the differences go way beyond mere outward appearances. The way the butterfly lives is totally contrary to the way the caterpillar lives. The caterpillar crawls on the ground. The butterfly soars in the sky. The caterpillar eats weeds. The butterfly drinks nectar from flowers. The caterpillar's purpose is to work and eat so that he can be turned into something else. The butterfly knows that she is already changed and lives to display her wondrous beauty.

And here is the main difference...

The butterfly knows who she is! She is no longer striving to become something better. She is now living a new life that outwardly expresses who she is on the inside.

The Kingdom Within

Like most things that are of God, we have taken this idea of the kingdom and turned it upside down. We apply it to us individually first and not corporately. But God works the other way around. He starts with the corporate and uses that to affect the individual. Obviously, the word "kingdom" implies a corporate group of people. There is a King and he rules over the "subjects" that live in his domain or realm. This realm is the place (and people) where he has complete control and he is the All in all.

The kingdom of God is within us (Luke 17:20, 21) because Jesus Christ *is* the kingdom. It is already here, in (and among) us. And our Lord prayed that this realm and culture that comes from the heavens would also come to this earth (Matt. 6: 10). He was praying here about a group of people who would live a different lifestyle than that of this world. They would be a people of the King. They would live their lives under his direct Headship and Lordship.

That lifestyle comes from within the life of Christ within each believer. The outward expression begins in the cocoon stage when the saints learn to lay down their lives for one another. A kingdom community is built within the cocoon. The self-centered, individualistic lives of the believers die to give way to the corporate life of Jesus Christ (John 3:30).

That kingdom is within you right now. But when did that kingdom come to live within you? Did it come in when you became a Christian? Did it come in when you were baptized? Did it come in when you went to church for the first time? Did it come in when you first heard the gospel?

Did it come in when you were born? Absolutely not! This kingdom came into you long before any of these events. This kingdom came into you before there was anything! This kingdom came into you before creation!

> *Then the King will say to those on his right*
> *hand, come, you who are blessed of my Fa-*
> *ther, inherit the kingdom prepared for you*
> *from the foundation of the world* (before cre-
> ation) (Matt. 25:34).

When the Father breathed his breath of life into you, that "spirit-seed" contained all the life of his Son. This "seed" was a part of his Son that existed since before eternity. That divine seed contains all that is in Christ. That includes his kingdom. If Christ lives in you, then so does his kingdom. That kingdom is a corporate or community life that is just waiting inside of you to come out.[1] That kingdom comes from the eternal realm (heavenlies) and yet it resides within your mortal flesh. That kingdom is the actual community life of the Triune God.

The Experience of the Kingdom

The kingdom of God is within you for a reason. It's because he wants to rule and reign upon this planet. First, he rules and reigns inside of you by you allowing him to be the Lord of everything in your life. He must have the preeminence in all things pertaining to you first (Col. 1:18). This does not mean that he is your first priority. It means that he is All. He is All in your family. He is All in your marriage. He is All in your career. He is All in your relationships. He is All in your finances. He is All in all. He is the center and substance and Lord of all things pertaining to you. It must start there, but it certainly can't end there.

---

[1]   See the author's book *The Community Life of God.*

Your experience of his Lordship must expand from you to others. Those whom you meet with as the church must also experience his Lordship together.

> *And He subjected all things under his feet and gave Him to be head over all things to the church, which is his body, the fullness of the One who fills all in all* (Eph. 1:22, 23).

Christ will not be the living practical head of the church unless he is head over each individual member of the body. This means that each one of us needs to learn how to draw our daily supply of life from the head. And then come together to seek his face for the direction of the church.

The question is this: is he just going to be the head of the church in theory or also in daily practice?

In the organic churches that I have been involved with, we made all decisions of the church by consensus. That means that there is no one person who made the decisions. We all came together and decided by consensus. We *all* agreed as to the mind of the Lord on a matter before we proceeded. If we don't all agree, then we wait until we do. Things move a lot slower this way, but we have found that we rarely ever miss God's direction.

He will move through different people at different times to accomplish what he wants. It won't always be the same people initiating things. But we all agree before we move ahead. In this way, he can be the practical and actual head of the church.

In the meetings, he is in charge. We seek him beforehand to find what he has given us to share with the saints.

Then anyone can share what the Lord has put on their heart whether it is a song, a poem, a testimony, a teaching, a revelation, or whatever. [2]

Of course, he is not just the head in meetings. He is the head of the church at all times and this needs to be true in our daily lives as well. As he directs each member, we call one another frequently to do things together. If a sister is going shopping, many times she will call another sister or two to go with her. If a brother is working on a project at home, many times he will call another brother to help him. We are learning to share our lives with one another, not just meetings.

Then this kingdom life within us should flow out to the world as well. We are learning to share the love and life that we have for one another with them. The life of the kingdom needs to be shared with those around us. There are believers and unbelievers alike that need to see the love of God displayed before them.

We have to step out of ourselves and step into Christ. Like putting on a pair of long overalls, we need to "put on" the Lord Jesus Christ (Rom. 13:14). And to do this we must step out of ourselves. We will do things we would normally never do when this happens. We might even corporately pray: "Lord, may your will be done, may your kingdom come; in our city as it is in heaven!"

---

[2]   For further reading on this subject please see the author's book *The Priesthood of All Believers.*

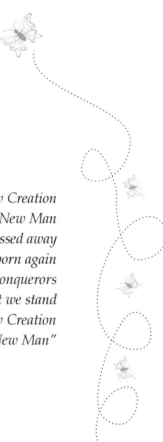

"We're a New Creation
We're a brand New Man
Old things have passed away
We've been born again
More than just conquerors
In Christ we stand
We're a New Creation
We're a brand New Man"

Pictures of the New Creation

There are many illustrations or "pictures" of our identity in the Scriptures. Most of these pictures speak of our oneness with Christ. In other words, most of these pictures are corporate. I would like to use this chapter to simply list and outline some of these beautiful pictures.

The Tree of Life

This Tree is found in three main places in Scripture: The Garden of Eden (Gen.), The New Jerusalem (Rev.), and one other place which is commonly overlooked. The Tree is found walking around the shores of the Sea of Galilee two thousand years ago! Yes, Jesus Christ said, "I am the True Vine and you are the branches" (John 15: 5a). This wonderful picture of our identity shows that we are one with him. It also shows that we are totally dependent upon him for all our supply of divine life. Apart from him, we can do nothing (John 15:5b).

The Tabernacle of Moses (See Exodus 25 - 30)

Everything in the tabernacle speaks of Christ and the church and I cannot go into much detail here. However, I can say that the Holy of Holies represents the head of the church, Christ himself. The rest of the tabernacle represents the enlargement or increase of Christ, which is his body, the church (Eph. 1: 22, 23).

The New Jerusalem (See Rev. 21, 22)

Everything in this city also speaks of Christ and the church. The gates of pearl are the entrance to the great city. This is his redemption. The streets are made of pure gold which always speaks of divinity in Scripture. The Tree of Life is in the city (vine and branches) and follows the River of Life (the fellowship of the Triune God). These both flow out from his throne.

Marriage (See Eph. 5:22-33)

Here again, this is our oneness with the Lord, our glorious Bridegroom (Eph. 5:23-32). The two have become one. Christ and the church have become one. This is the great mystery of the New Creation. How can two become one? How can a God who is one contain three Persons? Oneness is a mystery because we cannot understand it with our natural minds. Only God can reveal this to us.

The New Humanity (See Col. 3:9-11; Eph. 2:15; Eph. 4:24)

This is the whole Christ: the head and the body, the bridegroom and the bride, the vine and the branches. This is the new humanity and the one new person who is the corporate Christ. The New Creation is a new Person.

This new Person is our Lord and us. The birthplace of this new Person is the tomb where Jesus was buried. The birth date of this new Person is the day Jesus walked out of that tomb. The New Man was born on that day. In the resurrection, all of those who were crucified with him also rose with him as the One New Man - the New Creation.

The Wedding (See John 2)

The Lord's first miracle at the wedding of Cana is a "sign" of the new creation. The water being turned into wine is a wonderful picture of our transformation from a caterpillar into a butterfly. And this all happened at a wedding. Here again, we can see the Bridegroom and the Bride as another picture of the Great Mystery of our one-ness with the Lord.

There are many other pictures of the New Creation to be found in Scriptures. Your identity can be found all over that Book. Why not go on a treasure hunt yourself to see if you can find some?

Conclusion

Once Fred understood that he was not just a worm, but instead a wonderful caterpillar who contained the butterfly life within him, everything changed. Everything became brand new.

But first he needed to hear the good news. He needed to hear the truth about his own identity. He needed to not only hear it, but he also needed to *believe it.*

You can always tell when someone has *heard* truth but has not *believed* it yet. When you tell them who they are in Christ, they quickly respond with, "Yeah, I know that." When we respond so quickly and so glibly it's because that truth hasn't really become a part of us yet. We have not yet really believed. We have only assimilated intellectual knowledge.

Faith comes by hearing, but faith must follow. You hear, and then you believe. I have presented the truth of your real identity. I have done this by presenting your Lord. That's because he *is* your identity. You and he have become one.

Now, can you *believe* this? Now, dear branch of the Tree of Life, can you apprehend this? Now, dear holy and blameless one, can you step into your identity by faith? Now, dear chosen one, can you believe the truth of who you really are?

Fred was content to believe that he was a worm. And so his life continued to be that of a worm. Even though he heard the "good news" that he was really a caterpillar with Flyer life within him, he still chose to believe he was a worm. What a tragedy. To believe something that is just not true. To believe you are something much less than what you actually are. What a loss to the kingdom of God. What a loss to all those around you. What a loss to yourself.

The second tragedy is not believing who you are, and then, trying to become what you already are! This is the very core of religion. To try, in your own strength, to attain to a position you already have. To strive, in your flesh, to become the person that you already are. Discovery comes in realizing who you already are and what you already have.

You *already* are:

A saint
A holy one
Blameless
Chosen before creation
A son of the living God
His masterpiece
A new creation
A unique expression of him
Seated with him in heavenly places
A member of his body
In Christ
Blessed by God
A priest
A living stone in God's house
A son of the living God
His inheritance
The fullness of him

Part of his bride
A family member
And much, much more . . .
You *already* have:

The love of God
The grace and truth of Christ
The unsearchable riches of Christ
The life (DNA) of God
The down payment of God (Holy Spirit)
The spirit of revelation
The gifts and callings of God
The hope of glory
The treasures of wisdom and knowledge
The kingdom of God
Freedom in Christ
And much, much more . . .

And this is just a partial list of who you *already* are and what you *already* have. You are rich indeed. You are blessed indeed. Now you need to believe it. Then you will begin to see it. And then you will live it.

But remember that your individual identity is intricately tied into the corporate Christ. The life of the caterpillar, cocoon, and butterfly is a life together with your brothers and sisters. *You* are not the butterfly. *We* are the butterfly! God's eternal purpose is fulfilled in a corporate expression of his Son. And *you* are a very important part of that expression.

Butterfly for Freedom Flies

(tune: America the Beautiful)

Oh butterfly for freedom flies
For you have shed your skin.
Your beauty shines for all to see -
The Son of God within.

Oh butterfly, oh butterfly,
In grace you've made your way
And by the blood you are made new,
The old has passed away!

Oh butterfly in fledging flight
Your journey lies ahead
Through joyful times and wilderness
You shall be Spirit-led.

Oh butterfly, oh butterfly,
Remain as one and go
And show the world the love of Christ
Defeating every foe.

Oh butterfly hold up the torch
And see beyond the years
The hidden ones who search for Truth
Reach out and heal their tears.

Oh butterfly, oh precious one,
Because you have the Seed
The generation after this
Is waiting to be freed.

Linda Graff
January 13, 2007

Other books by Milt Rodriguez

The Coat of Many Colors
The Priesthood of All Believers
The Temple Within
The Community Life of God

Visit our website at:
www.therebuilders.org

For more information on organic churches
visit our website at:

www.housechurchresource.org

CPSIA information can be obtained at www.ICGtesting.com
Printed in the USA
LVOW01s0003310714

396760LV00032B/1524/P